The Starboard Quest

The Harmonic Battle Of Evermore

By

Mark Jager

Copyright page

Other works by Mark A. Jager

The Mystic Michigan Series
Mystic Michigander..
The Hidden Hand
The Tell-Tale Earth
Cryptic Michigan- Woodland Revelations
Cryptic Michigan- Epiphanies From Wonderland
The Starboard Quest- Sailing The Sea Of Sound To Explore Music's Connection To
The Universe
The Starboard Quest- Treasure Hunt

Zosma Publications

Table of Contents

Seven seas to sail

Welcome Aboard!

& seven notes to a scale.

Once upon a time, in a place not so far away, sailed a company of minstrels on the sparkling waters of the Aquarian age. Their harps were tuned to the music of the spheres, and their songs meandered from afar on the whispering wind. Perhaps if you listen very carefully, you can hear the faint echoes of their ancient songs returning to you on the crests of the universal tide.

The constellation Lyra is depicted as a celestial harp with
the wings of an eagle and is found in the sign of Sagittarius.

Researchers have discovered that all of the objects in the
solar system are heading towards Lyra
at a rate of twelve miles per second.

Introduction

⁂

Warning! Readers beware! Consider the possibility that there are unseen dark forces in this world that don't want you to discover the knowledge contained within these pages. Be prepared for interruptions and disturbances while reading them. Some of the information in this book comes from data that has been rescued from antiquity. It was found written in age-old books and scrolls that were tucked away in dusty, old depositories which ended up serving as time capsules.

Over the years, researchers have eventually found some of these old manuscripts and have been in the process of making them available to the public. If the darkness had had its way, some of the more vital material most likely would have remained hidden forever and would never have come to the light of public knowledge.

It has taken many centuries for some of this information to finally start getting out to enquiring minds. Many of the topics covered in this book have already been written about in former ages. It's just that much of the enlightening material was encapsulated in historic storehouses and forgotten about by people for hundreds of years. In fact, it seems almost as if this wisdom was hidden away on purpose and hermetically sealed to be kept secret for long extended periods of time. As if it had a mind of its own, it seems to have been awaiting the arrival of a specific type of people in a certain time period. Suddenly, these writings are coming into the awareness of specific individuals.

Have you ever seen the scenario sometimes depicted in motion pictures in which there were sacred and hidden vaults of ancient information, and in due season when the rays of specific stars came through an air shaft and shone a beam of light at a perfect angle on a hidden mechanism, a door would open into a lit vault containing cryptic earth changing information?

In a similar manner, It's as if we have arrived at the right time in history, and in a metaphorical manner of speaking, the stars have all shifted into the right places, shown their beams of light through the corridors of time, and now the doors of perception are slowly opening so we can gain access into a sacred citadel of sound. We excitedly delve into the arcane musical scrolls purposely left for us by ancient sages. It may be that the appointed time has come to decipher the mysterious musical hieroglyphics.

The Starboard Quest book series, and the soundtrack that goes with them are for a niche audience. They will only be understood by a certain type of people. They are designed for peculiar people who have a particular type of mindset. You may be one of the chosen few who are destined to have a copy of this book in your hands. If so, then as you read the books in this series, it's likely that the information contained in them will resonate with you.

If you are one of the people that the books in this series don't resonate with, then by all means put them down. In such a case, it is preferable for you to not read them. Truth is stranger than fiction, and if you are somebody who can't handle that fact, it's best for you to stay away from these books. You won't believe them anyway. Let them be reserved for the Royal Society of Stellar Musicians.

If you are one of the people who were destined to read this book and the others in the series, optimistically, this is what will happen while you read them. Hopefully a light will dawn in your consciousness. If in fact this does happen, a dynamic reality that has been right before you for your whole life, but has been hidden from you, could suddenly become apparent. The words of these books can come to life off of the pages. Or, perhaps what you read will mean nothing to you at the moment, but a realization of its contents will dawn upon you many years into the future. Either way, this book will have achieved its objective.

If this book does come alive to you, it will be because a certain type of light has shone on your mind. If it does, a hidden reality will become unveiled and light will break forth into your consciousness. A secretive musical realm will become visible. You will suddenly see this book living itself out right before the eyes of your mind.

Concealed musical wisdom from the past, and the visions that sages have had concerning a glorious new music of the future are delved into in this book. However, these ideas are not being shared with you so that you can live forever in the past, or dwell continuously in the future. Let the power and the musical epiphanies of the past, present, and future fully merge into your consciousness in the great reality of now. As the great poet William Blake once wrote, "To see a world in a grain of sand and a heaven in a wild flower, hold infinity in the palm of your hand and eternity in an hour."

Let the musical thoughts of all time, space, light, and sound amalgamate into your mind while you are reading. Through a unique, divine chemistry, may you be liberated from the musical darkness which attempts to encompass and envelope the world. Learn from the musical wisdom of the past, and get strength from the musical visions of the future and bring all of the hope and knowledge of all time periods into the present moment.

This information is meant to do good for you right now. That being said, you are free to believe or to not believe anything written in this book. This book is simply sharing unique musical ideas that have been presented throughout the centuries by various scribes, seers, and sages. You have to decide what you are going to take with you out of this book. It's alright to know what all of these various sages said, however, let your main goal be to receive divine wisdom directly into your inner being. No human being can give you that. That can only come from the Conductor of the symphony of all things himself. His is a wisdom far beyond all the sages who are quoted in this book. The purpose of quoting philosophers and sages is not to create a dependence on them. Hopefully, something they say will trigger the opening of many books in your own inner library.

Don't just accept what I have written in this book. Study these matters for yourself and see what benefit they have for you. I started out writing this book with a sarcastic attitude towards musicians playing toxic music, and towards people who discourage people with musical talent. Even though I have retained aspects of some of those bad attitudes, I also found that as I studied these topics I seem to have gone through a transformative process. I saw within both of these groups of people, my own shortcomings. There was and is a measure of the mistakes of both of these groups of people in me. None of us are perfect and forgiveness is the best policy.

Another point that came to my realization, is that at times I have had the same self centered problems that many artists have. Within the human condition is a tendency towards a musical superiority complex. There resides the tendency to tear down others in order to be personally elevated. In time, I developed more of an understanding of how, nobody wins unless we all win. I didn't begin writing with a large amount of knowledge about any of the topics in this book. I learned as I went. There are things worth sharing on these pages. I'm not an expert on this information and that's all there is to it. Remember, I'm just sharing what I've studied.

Although it may appear as if I have a large personal humanitarian concern for the human race and a desire to see them better utilize the great gift of music, keep in mind that I don't really have as great of a good will towards others as what I should have, and a large part of this endeavor has to do with my own personal interests, promotion and exaltation. I'm learning and hoping to be liberated from these types of attitudes. I'm not one hundred percent successful at that yet. Let's be up front about these things. Know this also. I'm not necessarily being friendly to you with this book. I may like you as a person, but at the same time I may be the enemy of your musical philosophies, tastes and undertakings. See me for what I am. If I perceive that people are purposely doing something wrong, there's a part of me that enjoys tearing them down.

As you read this book, and others in The Starboard Quest book series, please keep the following information in mind. Most of this knowledge is nothing new. Read this book from a perspective that you are learning from those in the past, but are bringing that understanding into the present moment. Some of the theories covered by this book may be pure conjecture. The non scriptural ideas from various sages may contain grains of truth, but are not necessarily the opinion or beliefs of the author. The ultimate goal would be to arise into reality beyond all musical conjecture and speculation.

On the other hand, people have sealed themselves off from understanding what people with different viewpoints than themselves have written about through the centuries. There's nothing wrong with understanding what other people have believed and written about through the centuries about music. Very simply put, the ideas of sages such as Pythagoras, Plato, Socrates, etc. are not considered to be equal to the Biblical truths, but it is recognized that there are grains of truth in them as well. This is simply an informative book. View it the same as what you might view a High School history book which presents the ideas of a very wide spectrum of religions, cultures, beliefs, and mindsets. There are scholars quoted in this book, who are and were involved with groups, associates, and beliefs that I personally would have nothing to do with. Just because I quote certain people when they give a great insight doesn't mean that I condone or support everything they believe or proclaim. Just because I quote certain historic people in this book, doesn't mean I'm encouraging you to read everything they've ever said or written. However, if they have a good point, they have a good point.

Before you climb aboard to read the chapters of this book, let the words of Argentinian philosopher Risieri Fronbdizi ring clearly in your mind. "The essence of the moral reformer and of the creator in the field of the arts lies in not adjusting to the predominant norms, or tastes, but unfurling the flag of "what ought to be" over and above people's preferences." I would ask that everyone reading this book would keep this quote in mind. There will be elements of truth presented in this book that you may not like. If you don't want to hear about it, don't read this book.

The Symbolism of The Starboard Quest

For those of you who are unfamiliar with the Starboard Quest book series, here's a short background on some of the symbolism used in the books. Emblems and symbols are used to aid the reader in understanding the major ideas of the books.

The main symbol of the book series is a ship. This ship is called "The Starboard Quest." You, as a reader, are symbolically climbing aboard this "ship" to embark upon a journey. The main goal is to discover the source of the secrets of music. The waves, on which this musical ship sails, are sound waves. You are traveling on an ocean of sound. Your fellow passengers on this ship consist of a large number of musical sages who have taught us many amazing things about music through the centuries. These passengers are those who have aimed for order, precision, and equilibrium with their music throughout the ages. In the deep past stand the shadowy figures of the originators. Through the symbolism of this book you will be sailing with them into the ever increasing revolving splendors of the music of the spheres.

The art of celestial navigation shows us that in order to reach our destination we have to learn to follow the laws of the heavens. Our symbolic ship is navigating by celestial navigation. In a similar manner, in order to reach our musical destination, we have to learn to follow the laws of the heavens as well. The constellation our ship is navigating towards, is the constellation Lyra. Lyra is an actual constellation. It is depicted by a huge celestial harp. The process of the ship navigating towards this constellation is symbolic of the quest to attempt to discover a higher form of elevated music. The ultimate destination, however, is beyond Lyra.

On this symbolic sea, let us imagine that there are other ships sailing on it as well. Some of them are occupied by musical pirates. The musical pirates are symbolic of those sailing on the sea of sound who are using dissonant tunings, frequencies, and rhythms. As universal archetypes go, pirates are easy to spot most of the time. They are known for their obnoxious loud ways, many of them wear earrings, tattoos, and use profanity just as a typical pirate would. Some of these pirates are actually pretty good at heart despite their ways. Although there is a type of musical battle ongoing, the idea is to rescue the pirates that may be good hearted off of their ships of disharmony and invite them aboard the ship which is in search of perfect harmony. With this picture story in mind, let's sail forward now on our quest to have a greater understanding of the mystical qualities of music. Onward! Anchors away! Into the deep blue.

Chapter 1

Harmonic and disharmonic beings

Why do some music notes sound naturally harmonious to human beings, while others sound naturally dissonant? This is a question that the great astronomer Johannes Kepler once asked himself. He came to the same conclusion that many others did. That is, that human beings recognize harmonious or dissonant musical notes by natural instinct. It seems to be a built in ability.

The ability to discern between harmonious and the dissonant sounds is apparently an inborn instinct which is preprogrammed into human beings. From earliest infancy, we seem to recognize harmony. Babies react to music at an early age. This is not a learned behavior. It is an innate reaction. That's not to say there aren't also some learned behaviors as well.

Some believe that the ability to distinguish between harmony and disharmony actually has its roots in deeper spiritual connections. When we see infants reacting to music, it's almost as if they're familiar with it. How are they familiar with it? Did they hear it in the womb and become familiar with it? Or is their recognition of music due to something beyond what we can comprehend? Are infants demonstrating some kind of a musical code from their DNA when they display natural reactions to music? Or, do the roots of their musical reactions have their origins in some place beyond the material universe?

Kepler recognized natural harmony in the minds of human beings. He didn't see it as learned behavior. He believed it to be innate. This is not the only place he found harmony. When he aimed his telescope at the starry heavens, he found musical harmony in the spacing and mathematical movements of the stars. He studied the stars and reported that musical mathematical ratios are present in celestial spheres. He very carefully recorded and preserved his universal musical information. His stellar findings can still be studied today.

Albert Einstein once said that human beings are, "slowed down light and sound waves, a walking bundle of frequencies tuned into the cosmos." In other words, we as human beings are directly infused into the principals, powers, and magnetic tides of the universe. We are directly integrated into its unseen forces. We are affected by gravity, electromagnetism, and many other forces. Most of these powers and forces are distributed through outer space.

For instance, the sun produces magnetism and electricity. On Earth, we live in a sea of magnetic energy which comes from the sun and from other stars. This magnetic energy is directly connected to the human body. This energy has been photographed by kirlian photography in scientific laboratories and has been shown to be surrounding the human body. We know it as an aura. This electrical field which surrounds the human body has its roots in space. If the mysterious cosmic energies of the galaxy were not being gracefully poured out upon us from the stars at this very moment, we would die. Without cosmic rays moving through us, our bodies are useless. Just as your phone or the appliances in your home are useless without electricity moving through them, so are our bodies useless without the cosmic rays of space moving through them.

Invisible stellar beams are passing through the very room which you are now occupying. We live in a world of energy waves. We currently stand at the center of a magnificent complex of forces and energies. The air which surrounds you is a conduit of powers. As you read this book, surrounding you is a unique chemistry of universal factors. Even as the seasons change around you, it is because thousands of miles from you planets and stars are moving around. The botany life outside your window is responding to forces in the Earth's magnetic field. As human beings, we have inner tides and outer tides. They are connected to magnetism. As was once mentioned by Thomas Aquinas, it is ridiculous to think that the moon, which pulls the whole tide of oceans, affects only the water in the oceans. As you look out into the night sky and observe billions of shining orbs, what you are witnessing is a vast energy system which exhibits a controlled distribution of energy. Consider the fact that every song you hear has its own magnetic field. In fact, this book has a magnetic field. Perhaps you will feel a magnetic field strengthening you as you read this book.

Musical ratios are found within space, and there is evidence that our bodies are ingrained with the same musical ratios. This scientifically proven energy which moves the universe, moves in specific mathematical sequences which resemble the mathematical patterns of music. The energy that animates our physical bodies moves in similar patterns. Our bodies are nourished by the stellar energy of the sun.

Since we are speaking of the musical ratios found in space, and also the musical ratios found in the human body, let's examine just a few of these ratios. First, let's explain what a musical ratio is. If you understand fractions, you can understand musical ratios. When you pluck a string on a guitar, or when a hammer within a piano strikes one of its internal strings, what happens? The string that is plucked or hit begins to vibrate. When it vibrates at a certain rate, it produces a certain tone. When it is vibrating, it is oscillating back and forth a certain number of times per second.

Let's say a string on a guitar is struck and it is vibrating at a rate of 300 times per second. Then, you strike a second string, and it is vibrating back and forth 200 times per second. The ratio between the two notes is 300/200. That can be simplified to 3/2. A 3/2 ratio in music is called a perfect fifth. Or, say perchance that one string is vibrating 400 times per second and producing a certain music note and another is vibrating 300 times per second and producing a different note. The difference between these two notes is 400/300, or 4/3. This ratio in music is called a perfect fourth.

Now that you understand this, let's give a few examples of how these same musical ratios are shown through planetary movement. The planet Pluto takes longer to orbit the sun than the planet Neptune. For every three orbits that Neptune makes around the sun, the planet Pluto only orbits the sun twice. This is a ratio of 3/2, which is the ratio of a perfect fifth in music.

Here is another example. Two of Saturn's moons exhibit a musical ratio to each other. The moon, Titan, orbits Saturn once every 15.94542 days. The moon Hyperion orbits Saturn once every 21.27661 days. This is a ratio of 4/3 which is called a perfect fourth in music. One further example would be the following. In music there is a term called, unison. Unison is a one to one ratio. The moon of planet Earth demonstrates this ratio in relation to the Earth. For every time that the moon orbits the Earth, it rotates exactly one time. This in musical terms demonstrates unison. This is a 1/1 ratio. If one were to spend their whole life doing nothing but writing down perfect musical ratios found within the mathematical fabric of the universe, they wouldn't be able to write them all down in many lifetimes.

Now let's give a few examples of how these same ratios are found in the human body. We have just taken a brief glimpse into how infants demonstrate musical awareness and connection through their behavior. Now let's take a look at how musical intervals can be found in the growth of a child.

There are musical ratios that can be found in the proportional relationships demonstrated by the size of a child's head in comparison to its body as it grows. At the moment of conception, a child is all head, which is a 1/1 ratio. A ratio which in musical terms is called unison. When an embryo is approaching its stage as a fetus, its head is one-half the size of its body. At two and a half months it becomes a fetus. While it is at this point of its development, its head is half the size of its body. This is a ½ ratio, and in music a ½ ratio is the ratio of an octave. At this point, it's gone from being an embryo to a fetus. It's reached a new "octave".

When a child is in the womb and is three months old, its head is one-third the size of its body. This means its body is ⅔ the size of its head, This is a ⅔ ratio , which in music constitutes a perfect fifth. At birth the baby's head is one-fourth the size of its body. This means the body is a ratio of ¾ in relation to the head, and in music a ¾ ratio is a perfect fourth. Birth is a new octave.

Then, when the child is two years old, its head is one-fifth the size of its body. Its body is ⅘ the size of its head. A ⅘ ratio in music constitutes a Major Third. When the child turns 12 years old, its head is one-seventh the size of its body. Its body is a ratio of 6/7 to the size of the head. A 6/7 ratio in music constitutes a septimal Minor Third. Finally, when the child becomes an adult and is fully grown, its head is one-eighth the size of the body. Which of course means that the body bears a ⅞ relationship to the head.

Author Armin Husemann, in his book entitled, "The Harmony of The Human Body" explains the growth of human beings in terms of the diatonic musical scale as follows: "What happens in (the growth of) human beings when the octaves ½, ¼, and ⅛ sound? The first octave sounds between the original sphere and the first whole number embryonic stage. As we saw, this octave, with which the whole melody begins, is connected with procreation. Through which the body emerges from the cosmic-female head (head grows to ½ the size of the body). The second octave is reached with the birth of the physical body (head grows to ¼ the size of the body by birth). Embryonic development has reached its conclusion when the baby is born. This "concluding point" is an aspect of our experience of the octave which is also relevant in the third octave. That is when growth stops." Growth stops when the head has grown to be ⅛ the size of the body. Therefore, within this sequence of growth, three octaves and the corresponding musical fractions are demonstrated. These are ½ which is an octave, ¼, and ⅛.

To clarify that a bit, let's put it this way. As has just been mentioned, certain researchers have compared the growth of a baby all the way from conception to full adulthood to musical scales. In this particular way of thinking, each major stage in the development and growth of a human being is considered a new octave. In music, a new octave is a new beginning. The old scale is gone and the new one begins. In the growth of a human being, there are various stages of growth some have called these stages "octaves."

In this line of thinking, conception is considered to be a new octave. It brings an end to the original time in the spirit world, and marks the beginning of a whole new form of existence, or, as they may call it, a new octave. The soul in the body has come into a new sphere, into a new plane of existence. This is what they call the first octave.

Then the embryo grows through all of its stages of development, it becomes a fetus and continues up the scale and when the fetus reaches its highest state of development it comes to birth. It is now ready to enter another new sphere, which has been referred to as another new octave. This has been called the second octave. As has been mentioned earlier, at each stage along the way the mathematics of musical proportions are clearly demonstrated by the growth of the body.

After birth, the human being continues to climb up the scale from stage to stage until it reaches full adulthood. When growth is complete, it has come to the third octave. Once again, the mathematics of musical proportions can be found within the growth of the body.

It's interesting that researchers have found and are continuing to find many different musical ratios built right into the human body and the universe. These discoveries have been ongoing for hundreds of years. However, at this point in history, the understanding seems to be accelerating. Science seems to be indicating a direct connection between mathematics, music, proportions of the human body, and the universe. Is there any evidence that people in various cultures from thousands of years ago believed in the connection between man, music, and the universe?

Some of the deepest religious and philosophical thinkers who have ever lived, have had an unshakable belief in highly elevated musical beings.These beings lived in the spirit world and had powers which were greater than the powers of human beings. These musical beings were harmonious but some became disharmonious to divine order. This idea is not found in just one religion, but in a number of them. These beliefs continue to be a part of various faiths to this day.

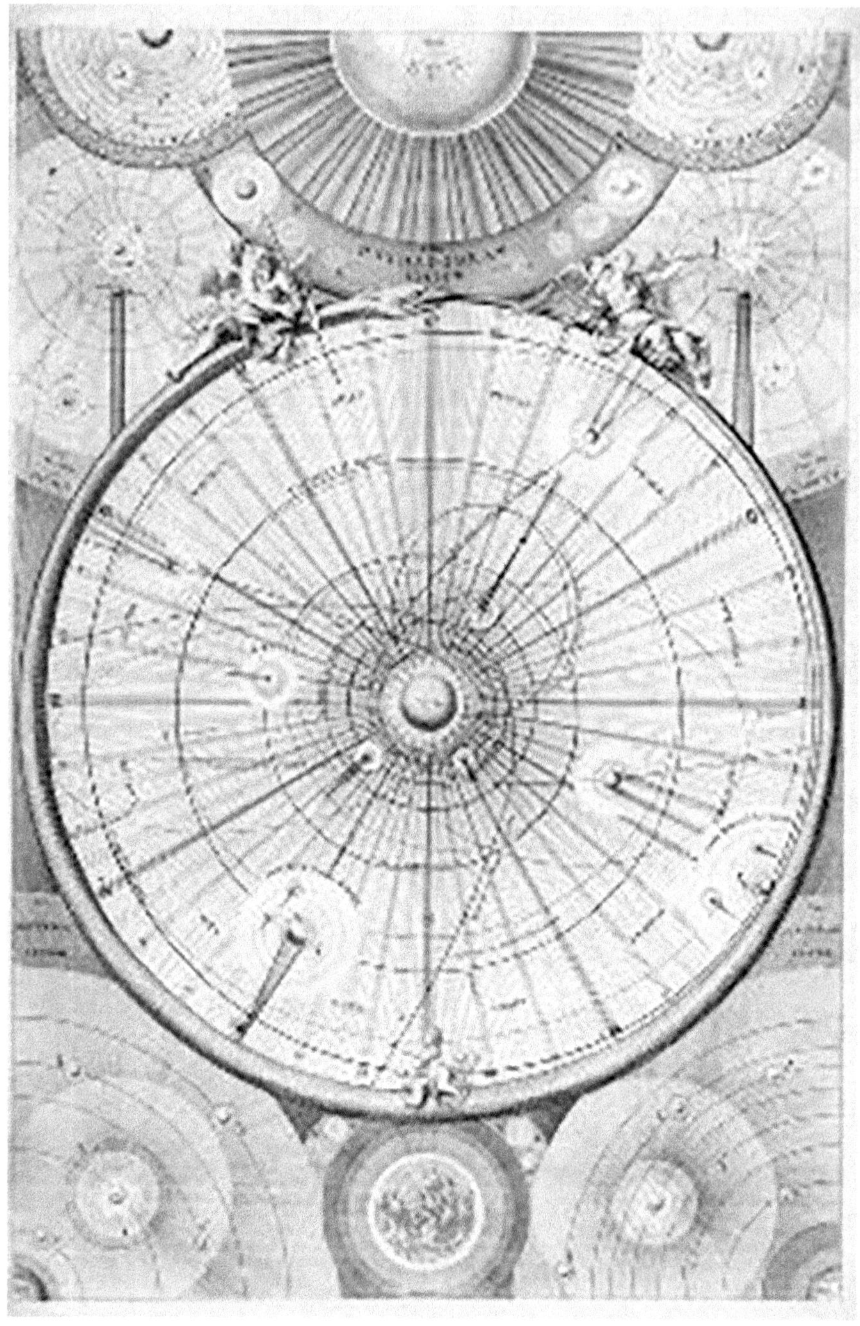

In ancient times there was a prevailing belief among various cultures
that exalted celestial beings overseen the music of the spheres.

Even in stories which were written outside of the realms of religion, we find various cultures writing stories which, when more closely examined, depict the idea of divine musical heroes and sinister musical villains. Where do these concepts come from? How did the ideas originate? Ancient sages placed religious value on these ideas, and gave a sacred place to music in nearly every culture. Why was music deemed so significant? Why was music considered to be so important back then, whereas, in the modern day many see it as just a childish pastime good for nothing but foolish entertainment?

Ancient cultures developed elaborate musical systems which stressed the importance of having orderly music in their societies. They went to such meticulous lengths trying to instruct people how to play orderly and harmonic music that to some modern people it seems absurd. Why the overkill? Were they just bored? Did they have nothing more important to do? In many cultures the people struggled to survive. How did they find the time to develop such orderly and strategic music standards? Many of them even had musical priests in their societies. Why did they find this necessary? By modern standards, this really seems strange. Were they ignorant? Or, did they know something that most of the human race forgot a long time ago?

In what ways did ancient cultures appear to go to extremes with the idea of orderly music in their societies? The Greeks were a good example of what is being spoken of here. Some researchers claim that in ancient Athens, if a musician or songwriter produced a dissonant or disharmonious piece of music they could be arrested or exiled from the country. To write an inharmonious piece of music was considered a crime against humanity. In other words, the person creating unharmonious music was considered a musical villain. What were the Greeks basing their logic on?

Socrates, the brilliant philosopher, went on record saying that in order for a utopian society to ever be realized, a society must first be purged of its toxic music. What was considered toxic music? He believed that if you want this world to be great, you've got to get rid of its unprincipled music. They saw music that didn't meet their standards as being noise pollution which plagued society. How did they know? Who made them the judge? What were they basing their ideas on? The Greeks were very intelligent about many things. Modern civilization is based on many of their ideas. However, when it comes to their high standards for music, the Greeks are largely ignored. Why are these standards ignored, when so many of their standards in other areas of life have become interwoven into our modern life?

Years later during the Protestant reformation, we hear Martin Luther echoing some of these ideas, and taking them a step further. In his opinion, not only was it necessary to get rid of toxic music, but it was also vital that music be completely taken away from perverted musicians and placed into the hands of those who would try to do what was right with it. Here is a man who was indirectly responsible for helping to bring about the renaissance, which was made possible by the reformation. The Catholic Church had suppressed the arts in many ways and the reformation liberated the creativity of the people and helped bring on the Renaissance.

Why were sages, philosophers, and theologians so concerned about musical order? It may seem like a departure from the topic of music, to venture for a short moment into the medical field. However, if you are patient, you will find out how researchers during the renaissance connected the order and harmony of the universe and music with physical health.

In 1493, one year after Columbus had discovered America, a child was born in Switzerland. His name was Theophrastus Bombastus von Hohenheim. He was later to be known as Paracelsus. Paracelsus was a physician, chemist, theologian, and philosopher of the German renaissance. He brought about an awareness that had to do with the subjects of harmony and disharmony, in relation to spiritual, mental, and physical well being.

Paracelsus was 10 years younger than Martin Luther. He grew up during the Protestant reformation. As people were becoming liberated from the restrictions of Catholicism, he was free to explore many unconventional medical cures. He had such revolutionary ideas in the field of the medical arts that he was called the Martin Luther of medicine. He strongly opposed the Catholic church, which tried to suppress many of his cures. He is known as the "father of toxicology". He was one of the first medical professors to state that Doctors needed to have a knowledge of which chemicals to prescribe to help treat illness. At that time, doctors believed that removing the blood from people cured them. Paracelsus said that herbs and chemicals were healing remedies. Many of the leaders of the Catholic church thought of him as a crazy heretic.

Paracelsus had the belief that every star in the sky had a counterpart in a plant on Earth. Each of the stars were radiating rays of light which helped or hindered people. The word "influenza" means, "to be planet-struck, afflicted as if by an evil star." To a certain extent, it was believed that illnesses were in part caused by stellar light striking a person at the wrong angle at the wrong time. Illnesses were considered a disaster. The word "disaster" has its roots in the meaning of "the unfavorable position of a planet or star".

Paracelsus believed that certain botanical plants on Earth were absorbing particular stellar rays. These stellar rays each contained a certain cymatic pattern. As the plants were absorbing those certain cymatic energy patterns, they stored them. A person, who was out of harmony with the universe and had gotten ill as a result of being out of harmony, could get back into harmonic equilibrium by absorbing the nutrients, or cymatic patterns of stellar energy stored in the plants.

Paracelsus believed that the entire universe is a well ordered organism. He saw all of the interrelated parts of the entire universe, as well as the unseen forces which moved the planets as a single organism, a vast harmonic structure. He saw nature as an orderly system that followed the unseen laws and patterns of space.

Paracelsus believed that illness was, in part, the result of getting out of harmony with the orderly movement of the tidal forces of the cosmos. He had a belief that human beings were supposed to live in harmony with Divine will. He looked at the night sky, saw the orderly heavens, and believed that the universe was an expression of that perfect Divine will. He could observe the effect that star light (most obviously the sun) had on plant life. He recognized that when people ate plants, herbs, and other healing substances, they were absorbing energy that came from the sun, or in other words, from a star. It occurred to him that it wasn't just the rays of the sun that struck the earth, but the stellar rays of many different stars. Plants absorbed these stellar rays both directly from starlight, and from minerals in the ground which actually stored these same stellar energies.

Each organ, or part of the human body has been scientifically proven to have its own measurable frequency. When there was a problem within the human body, Paracelsus implied that that particular part of the body had fallen into disharmony. Therefore, it had fallen out of harmony with the universe at large. Therefore, if you could find the plant that was absorbing that particular frequency from its designated star, and absorb that particular cymatic energy pattern into your body, it would help you heal. Plants are following an unseen schematic or pattern as they grow. It was believed that by absorbing that energetic pattern into your body, you could heal. Ironically, it is now coming into human awareness that certain plants, shaped in a certain way, will actually heal body organs and parts that are shaped in a similar way. Why? They both function and are shaped by the same energetic patterns.

How the patients of Paracelsus were healed by eating certain plants, or by taking certain chemicals, was thought of in terms of the following verbal illustration. If you take two tuning forks which are similar in pitch, and you strike one of them, the other fork of similar pitch will begin to resonate with the other one even though it has not been struck. This is called harmonic resonance. So, if you were to eat a certain plant which was in harmonic resonance with a certain part of the body, you could heal that part of the body.

It can be observed that some plants open up to the rays of the sun, and other plants open to the rays of the moon. It is known that the stars affect the growing seasons. This has been demonstrated for many years by the uncanny accuracy of the farmers almanac. Ben Franklin first published Poor Richard's Almanac in the 1700s. It is reported that George Washington used the almanac to maintain his plantations. It is reported that in Colonial times, farmers wouldn't even think about farming without one. Farmers have planted by certain phases of the moon for centuries. It is obvious that the cosmic rays of space affect biological life on Earth, just how much they affect biological life isn't entirely known. It makes sense that being in harmony with the universe is essential.

If you can understand this concept, it is easy to understand why ancient sages wanted to base the mathematics of their music systems and scales on the orderly mathematics of space. This may also help explain why ancient societies were so concerned about having orderly music that worked with the laws of nature rather than against them. They had the belief that disharmony in music provoked physical ailments. On the other hand they believed that harmony in music encouraged health and well being.

How did musical sages of the past determine what music was harmonic? Where did they look for the answers? To the heavens. The Chinese based their music systems on the precise movements of the stars of the zodiac. Anything that varied from the mathematical order of the entrancing heavens was considered dangerous. They believed that if enough people began playing disorderly music, the entire empire would begin to disintegrate. In ancient China, oriental authorities monitored their provinces to see what kind of music the people were playing and what tuning they were playing in. if they were playing the wrong kind of music,in the wrong tuning, the people in that province were considered ill and in need of healing.

Where did they come up with this idea? Is there any evidence that this was true? Furthermore, what constitutes harmonious music? What elements in modern music, or in music in general should be kept? Which elements should be eliminated? The answers seem complicated. Modern musicians have found it easier to just ignore these types of questions. Should we ignore them? Or would it be wise to at least consider the basic musical ideas brought to us by some of the most brilliant men who have ever walked the face of this Earth? How can we, in this time period, make an attempt to meet these standards? Is it even possible?

To find answers, as to why the Greeks, Hebrews, Orientals, Egyptians and other cultures placed such orderly and strict requirements upon their music, we may have to go further back in history. Our journey will take us back to sacred texts and to some of the foundational beliefs of at least three Abrahamic religions. There is a common thread that runs through many different cultures. This thread consists of the common belief they had which consisted of the idea of there being musical heroes and villains. Perhaps studying ancient texts will give us an idea as to why they placed such disciplined standards on their music.

Chapter 2

An Ancient War

Throughout the centuries, artists have often depicted angels as advanced musical beings. They have been portrayed as elevated musicians, playing harps, and trumpets. Millions of people all over the world from various religions and cultures believe that these exalted, otherworldly singers and musicians still exist. It is believed that these beings still play music in realms hidden to man. It is said that at times, some of this music has briefly meandered into our world and has been heard by the ears of mortals.

This painting by William Blake depicts a time before the ages of the world when the morning stars sang together. Notice the celestial beings in the sky above the Earth.

Major religions have spoken of unearthly music. The ancient Chinese believed in cosmic tones that were involved in the creation of the universe. Buddhists see vibration as a sacred and important force. Hindus believe the universe was created by sound. What is the foundation for these beliefs? Where did they come from? Why do they all seem to have similar ideas?

In Christianity, there is the understanding that angelic beings play symbolic instruments that are either directly connected to, or run in tandem with titanic forces that are unleashed on Earth. Such is the case in the book of Revelations where angelic beings are depicted as sounding trumpets as mysterious events are enacted upon the Earth. It doesn't necessarily imply that the musical instruments cause the events, however, they are associated with the events. It is true that the book of Revelations is a symbolic book, and the trumpets are often spoken of as being emblems by those discussing them. Either way, it's interesting that musical instruments are used in the symbolism. In the book of Revelations, the 24 elders around the throne of Deity all have harps they are playing. They are all musicians.

In a whole realm of study outside of religion, in mythology, the Greeks had stories of benevolent musical spirits called "muses". They also believed in an exalted musical being named Orpheus who had power over the physical elements through sound. There are ancient people who believed that the universe was sung into existence. The Greeks connected each of their seven musical modes to various houses of the zodiac. This shows that they believed in a connection between stellar harmony, order, and music notes. This belief was similar to the beliefs of the Chinese.

In a brief summary, it is interesting to note that a large number of cultures agree that there are divine musical beings, and it is at least implied by many of them that music is associated with some of the most powerful forces in the universe. Is there something that can be learned through this common musical thread that runs through the world's major religions as well as in the stories from various cultures?

The story continues, all of the Abrahamic religions share a further common belief. They all believe that there was once a place where exalted and advanced musical beings lived and sang together. It was a divine civilization of universal order, harmony, and equilibrium. Their environment was harmonious, and it was highly likely that their music reflected that atmosphere of perfect harmony.

This "harmony" which we are considering,was universal harmony. It was harmony between them and their Creator. It was a harmony between beings. Perfect harmony in communication and purpose. A Perfect balance in every aspect of their faith civilization. It was a harmony and equilibrium of all things. It reached far beyond just musical harmony, but most likely included it.

All of the Abrahamic religions share the belief that at a certain point, warfare broke out between two groups of highly exalted beings in this place of perfection. They are seen as having abilities beyond human beings and one of their areas of divine ability as has been previously mentioned, is in the realm of elevated musical capacity.

In the ancient texts of scripture, very little is revealed about the nature of this war. It is known that a musical being with musical instruments built right into him became spiritually disharmonious and led one-third of the beings into a rebellion against divine authority. The "disharmonious" rebels sought to bring disorder and upset the equilibrium. They wanted to take over so they brought about a rebellion against authority.

Lucifer is spoken of as leading one-third of the beings in this rebellion. It is symbolized in terms of him taking down one-third of the stars of heaven. This is interesting because stars are often symbolic of universal order and harmony. The rebellious spiritual beings tried to upset the harmonic balance of their faith civilization. They wanted to take over.

What is interesting is that there is no mention of there being any casualties in this war. We are told that good angels cast them out, but we aren't told if they used weapons or what kind of weapons they were using if they did use weapons. In Isaiah 14:11 it mentions that the "noise" of Lucifer's viols was cast down with him. It doesn't even call what he did with his instrument music, it simply refers to it as "noise." Here the universal idea of a musical villain appears. A villain who makes "noise".

Chapter 3

Music as a Force to repel Evil

We find that in ancient times there was a belief that the right kind of music could repel evil spirits. This is shown in the account of David driving evil spirits away from King Saul by playing his harp for him. This event is found in the Hebrew scriptures. In other Jewish writings such as the Talmud, the belief that the Hebrew people had concerning the heavenly origins of sacred music are revealed. For instance, it is written in the Talmud that King David had a harp hanging over his bed. On certain instances at midnight, the north wind would blow through a window into the palace. The wind would strike the harp and the harp would play without being touched by human hands. The old testament speaks of receiving songs in the night.

The Jewish Talmud states that King David had a harp that hung over his bed. At midnight, the north wind would blow through a window, strike his harp, and the harp would play on its own accord.

The Jewish people believed in divine music, but this type of thinking also made its way into Christianity. Consider the following words of Charles Spurgeon in the 1800s. "Night is the time of terror and alarm to most men and women. Yet even night has its songs. Have you ever stood by the seaside at night, and heard the pebbles sing, and the waves chant God's glories? Or have you never risen from your bed, and opened your bedroom window and listened? Listened to what? Silence- except now and then a murmuring sound, which seems like sweet music. And have you not imagined that you have heard the harp of God playing in heaven? Didn't you conceive, that the distant stars, those eyes of God, looking down on you, were also lips of song- that every song was singing God's glory, singing as it shone, its mighty maker, and his lawful, well deserved praise? Night has its songs. We don't need much poetry in our spirit to catch the song of the night, and hear the planet and stars as they chant praises which are loud to the heart, though they are silent to the ear- the praises of the mighty God, who holds up the arch of heaven, and moves the stars in their courses". There have been many others in the Christian faith such as Billy Graham who wrote that there is a future music coming which far surpasses anything on Earth. This heavenly music is believed to have the power to cast out evil spirits.

In the 1800s, Charles Spurgeon went on record about the music of the spheres and of nature.

The belief in sonic exorcisms was spoken of in the middle ages by reformer and songwriter Martin Luther. Luther said, "Music is hateful and intolerable to the Devil. I truly believe and do not mind saying that there is no art like music, next to theology, that can calm the agitations of the soul, which plainly shows that the Devil, the source of anxiety and sadness, flees from the sound of music as he does from religious worship". Notice that Luther said that music drives evil away. He didn't say that noise does. Therefore, music is to be contrasted to the idea of "noise" such as what was cast out of a place of perfect harmony along with Lucifer and his band of angels.

If one is to consider the fact that over a period of thousands of years, there has been the belief in several religions that music can be used as a tool for the divine to move through to cast out evil spirits, it begs the question; Where did this belief originate? Ask yourself the question of whether this belief and practice originated on Earth, or in another dimension, heaven? Were human beings the first to have this knowledge and use this power? Or, was this power first implemented by elevated musical beings called angels? We don't know. Consider this question and meditate on it.

Here is another question to consider. If it is noted in the scripture that divine power can move through music being played by a human being on a man made instrument, then what may be possible through the music of a sinless, angelic being playing on an instrument divinely and supernaturally constructed? The Shepherd boy David, having been given this wisdom and ability, used it to repel evil spirits. Would an angel, with far greater musical ability than a human, sit idle and not use his musical ability to do the same? This is a further question for you to ponder.

In the Dead Sea scrolls was found an ancient inspired writing called "The Book Of Enoch". In this ancient text, Enoch is taken to another dimension, and there he sees spiritual beings who are described as being an army. In a particular portion of the text, this is how he describes them; "In the middle of heaven I saw armed troops, worshiping the Lord with tympani and pipes and unceasing voices, and pleasant voices, and pleasant and unceasing and various songs, which it is impossible to describe. And every mind would be quite astonished, so marvelous and wonderful is the singing of these angels. And I was delighted listening to them."

What is very interesting is, in this portion of the text, the spiritual beings are described as being armed troops. In the next sentences nothing is described that can be recognized as a conventional weapon of war, that human beings would recognize as a weapon. Instead, it is mentioned that they are carrying musical instruments around and singing. This is also something for the reader to think about.

Chapter 4

Archetypes- How History Repeats Itself and runs In Cycles

Some who have read so far may be of the opinion that these religious stories are interesting, but how does that relate to the modern study of music? Let's leave the religious study for a moment and venture into the study of music from the perspective of psychology. Let's examine human consciousness and talk about Carl Jung, and the human mind with its archetypes and subconscious symbolism.

What is an archetype? Generally, it is an original model from which something is developed or made. In a literary setting, it's those images, figures, character types, settings, and story patterns that, according to the Swiss analytical psychologist Carl Jung, are universally shared by people across all cultures.

These same patterns play themselves out over and over in books, theater, and even in real life. These archetypes are deeply embedded in human consciousness at a universal level. Whenever you see a certain archetype coming up over and over across many cultures over long extended periods of time, it's not an accident. These archetypes are surfacing through the subconscious minds of people within the vast ocean of the collective consciousness.

These emblematic designs are real. They aren't fabricated. In regards to these real life archetypes, people can, at this very moment, be seen acting these archetypes out in physical matter, most of the time, without realizing they are doing it. The patterns first exist at an unseen level. These archetypes have been found regularly in literature and on certain occasions in real life throughout time. History repeats itself. Events and archetypal characters seem to run through history in cycles like clockwork. They are also known as types and shadows.

Also, if you look into literature and theater, as well as into the world of opera with its symphonic compositions you can see this psychology working itself out through a number of different mediums. They all seem to have reoccuring themes that play themselves out over and over despite the differences in the art forms expressing them.

Within the vast library of archetypes, you will find many different kinds, and some of them are the archetypes of musical heroes and musical villains. For example, Greek legends often speak of deceitful female musical creatures called sirens. Why do these types of images keep coming up from within the subconscious minds of humanity? Where do they originate before they find their way into the human mind? The human mind seems to be picking up on something that resides at a deeper level in the universe, or in other dimensions.

Sirens were spoken of as being beautiful women of powerful sexuality, whose beautiful singing voices lured sailors towards their deaths. These women were sometimes depicted as voluptuous mermaids. The Greeks represented them as bird-women. The sirens were said to dwell on an island, and would sing for sailors on their ships as they were sailing near the island. The sailors would sail their ships closer to shore to hear the singing of the talented women. Their attention would be so focused on the women that they would accidentally crash their ships into the rocks and sink their ships. In the stories, the shores were said to be littered with the dead bodies of the unfortunate victims of the sirens.

This is just a story of course, however, the idea behind these stories is that they are based on an archetypal pattern, and they contain a moral lesson. You be the judge. As you look out on modern society, do you see any female performers who could be considered to be the modern equivalent of them? Sure, men may not be crashing ships into rocks because of the singing of beautiful women, but, are there beautiful women in the music industry today that end up being the ruin of men? You answer this question for yourself.

Somewhere buried within the subconscious depths of the human race is a primal fear of evil musicians. This subconscious fear has found its way into stories told worldwide. It has found its way into many different stories. It is such a common fear that it may prompt one to ask, where, and what are its origins?

Here is the archetype of another musical villain. Many are familiar with the story of the Pied Piper. Most people have heard of the Pied Piper as this story is universal. The Grimm Brothers rendition goes like this; A flute playing piper dressed in bright clothing arrives in the town of Hamelin, Germany one day. He's charismatic, witty, and cheerful. He offers to rid the town of its rodent problem seeing as to how it has been overrun with rats. The Mayor says yes, and agrees to pay the piper if he gets rid of the rodents.

The piper goes through town and plays his pipe. The rats are hypnotized by his music and follow the sound out of town. The piper leads them to a river. The rats fall into the river and drowned. This charismatic musician, who everybody seems to love, appears to have done a great service for society. The piper, having rid the town of rats, expects to get paid. The Mayor refuses to pay him. The piper gets angry and vows revenge.

One day while the parents are all busy at church with their religion, the piper comes to town and enchants the children with his music. The children follow the piper as he leads them away from their town, their religion, and their parents. When the parents get out of church, the children are nowhere to be found. They are never seen again. There is actually some evidence found in inscriptions in the German town of Hamelin that seem to indicate that something just like this actually happened. This story is known universally. Are there any lessons to be learned from it? Once again, you be the judge, has anything happened within the scope of modern history that could be considered the equivalent of this archetype playing itself out once again?

These stories are said to be archetypical. There are also archetypes of musical heroes. One such hero in Greek culture was Orpheus. In this story, Jason and the Argonauts are depicted as sailing past the island of the sirens. While they were sailing by the island, they had Orpheus play his harp and sing. The musical skills of Orpheus were powerful enough that the sailors focused on his songs rather than on the singing of the sirens. The sirens were thereby defeated and the sailors continued on their mission of destiny. One thing to take note of here, is the fact that this was a whole island of sirens. There may have been thousands of them. It was one man on a ship against what may have been thousands. Thus, the archetype of a hero vastly outnumbered who is victorious against all odds. This story depicts a type of sonic battle between good and evil musicians.

In addition to that, what is even more interesting about archetypes, is that at times they can contain hundreds of components. These components all work together to play out the drama. Some of these archetypes require thousands of people to play the archetype out such as in the story just mentioned. All of the components work together to play out a scenario which often contains a moral lesson.

What is even more amazing, is that many times the people playing out the villain roles either have no idea that this is what they are doing, or they relish the idea of being evil. With some of these universal archetypes, evil has to come and set up its archetypal structure in order for the role of the musical hero to be made manifest. You see, in stories such as in the story told above, there had to be thousands of sirens singing on the island in order that the musical hero could sail past and defeat them. Although he was outnumbered, he defeated them against all odds.

Chapter 5

A further inquiry into archetypes.

If You looked out upon this world, and you knew what to look for, is it possible that you would see thousands of archetypes playing themselves out? The stories just mentioned are only a few of the best known. Since the topic of this book is music, let's take a look at a few different general types of villain archetypes and see if they can be applied to the modern world of musical performers.

Our discussion so far has pointed out that in sacred texts, and in the literature of ancient cultures, the idea of musical heroes and musical villains has often shown up. What constitutes a villian? There may be many different opinions about this, but for the sake of this study, let's examine some well known villain archetypes. These are actual, recognized villain patterns that have actually been categorized by researchers. If we were to take this catalog of villain archetypes, and apply them to modern musical performers, would there be any modern performers who would fit the description of any of the different types of villains?

The Classic Villain; The first type of villain we are going to look at is called the classic villain. Classic villains have very few redeeming qualities. They do bad things just because they want to. They are proud and public about the evil they do. They do bad things just because they're evil. They may even proclaim themselves to be the devil himself. They simply just don't care. They are there to try to foil the hero. They are openly rebellious, defiant, and immoral. This is a very well known archetype and if you were to look into the catalog of archetypes put together by people like Carl Jung, you would most likely find this archetype. So, you be the judge. Do you find those among modern musical performers who would appear to fit this archetypal pattern? If there aren't any, no one will come to mind.

The anti-villain: The next type of villain we are examining is the anti-villain. Anti-villains are actually bad guys who exhibit non-villain characteristics. In other words, they are considered "good guys", compared to the bad guys. They have noble traits, values, and goals. They have some of the ethics of heroes, but at the same time, lead people down a path of degradation and degeneration. For example, they may sing love songs and talk about world peace, but at the same time through their power and influence they lead people down a path of such detrimental things as drug use and other immoral behaviors that end up destroying people. Although having some noble traits, they, in the long run, are detrimental to society, even though they have done some good. You are the expert here. These are just simply generic definitions of different types of villains, and you are determining if anyone in the modern music business fits the archetypical descriptions.

Beast villains- Beast villains are just plain monsters. They rely on people's physical appetites and tendency towards self destruction to achieve their goals. They depend on people's animal instincts and depend on those people to empower them. In other words, they act just like animals and so do their followers.They may even sing songs talking about what animals they are. They bring the integrity of society down a notch. In doing so, and in encouraging others to do so, they are a detriment to civilization. As has been said before, apply this generic villain classification to the world of music performers. Are there any that seem to fit the bill?

The Authority Figure Villain- These are villains who have achieved a higher position of power than other villains. No matter how much power they get, they always crave for more. They may even receive honors and titles from the state. Their usual goal is domination. They may either have positions of political power, or have strong political influence. They may put on a real humanitarian face, and actually do some humanitarian things, but deep down their real goal is more personal power and even greater domination. The topic is archetypes. The subject is musical performers. Are there any that fit this archetype? If not, as has been said, no one will come to mind.

Henchmen Villains- Henchmen are villains who do a bigger villains bidding. They are sidekicks of a major villain. They have the same devious mindset, morals, and cravings as their masters, but don't have the brains and fame of them. Do you know of any musical performers who fit this description?

The Corrupted Villain- Corrupted villains are those who were once innocent and good, but turned evil. Dirty cops, crooked politicians, and shady business people fall into this category. Can you think of any modern musicians or recording artists that would fit this category? These would be those who started out sweet and innocent, but became more degraded and immoral as they became more famous. They were once pure, and have become bad, and now they are out to let the world know.

These are just a few of the archetypes. They are all universally recognized patterns. They have played themselves out throughout history and have been found in nearly every culture on earth. They are all recognized prototypes of evil. If there are musicians and performers that fit these descriptions, then they are playing the parts of musical villains. One of the most incredible things is, many of them say so themselves. They admit they are playing the part of a villain.

Quite often performers or recording artists will say, "that evil person you see me as, while I'm performing is not me. It's just a stage persona. I'm just playing a part." The performer will often admit that they are simply embodying an evil archetype. This is not surprising. There have to be a lot of them. Why? If you remember the story of how Orpheus was engaged in a musical battle with a whole island of sirens, you will recall that in order for the archetype of musical hero to be made manifest, thousands of villains needed to be put into place so they could all be defeated. Something is happening in the world right now that performers who are embodying the archetypes of villains don't comprehend yet. There's a much bigger picture that's in the process of emerging. It is the process of their eventual defeat.

Let's use our imaginations here for a moment. Let's say that there are actual archetypes of musical villains that have been playing themselves out right before our very eyes for decades. These 'villain archetypes have been given the freedom to develop their characters. How would this have been possible if there had not been free speech and expression? This may be why people are allowed to express something vile even though a large segment of the population is against it.

Although these types of behaviors and expressions are not being condoned by this writing, if you examine the idea of a musical archetype which has hundreds of components in its structure closely, you will see that it may be possible that what the musical villains of this time period are doing, is necessary. Many different people were and are allowed to express the villain patterns. It may have been because the villain pattern has to be in place before a greater hero pattern can be made manifest that supersedes it. As has been mentioned previously, a structure of musical villains needs to be in place so that the musical hero pattern can rise above it. The hero wins despite being vastly outnumbered. How can this archetypal scenario play itself out unless the villains are first in a position to make this archetypal scenario possible?

It may be true that a number of modern musicians exhibit some of the characteristics found in archetypal villains. It may also be true that ancient and modern religions have believed in highly advanced musical beings that went bad. What does that have to do with the music that is prevalent in the world now? These are all amazing facts about the past, but what do they have to do with the here and now? Consider the possibility that all of the musical villains of the past are just examples for you to learn from. Also, entertain the thought that if you looked hard enough you would find that these archetypes are still here in modern times. There is no reason that these patterns would not still be playing themselves out. They are universal.

When the possibility of there being musical archetypes is carefully examined, there appears to be a strong indication that thousands of modern musical villains have taken their place in a vast structure which appears to be working as a massive musical archetype. The musical components seem to have been carefully and meticulously arranged and set into place perfectly. Many performers have publically prided themselves in their evil stage personas and have declared themselves to be sinister archetypes.

This is all done in the name of entertainment, however, is there more truth to what they are saying than what even they realize? Is what we see happening in this world actually brought about by forces moving in the unseen world? When you see people acting out the roles of musical villains, are they simply becoming the embodiment of forces moving in the unseen world?

Remember, archetypes are predetermined patterns that play themselves out through many generations. They manifest in many cultures and in diverse ways. The cycle is always similar. The world in which we now live is only the visible hemisphere. The causal forces are in the invisible hemisphere.

It would certainly seem as if we have been watching an incredible musical drama unfold before our very eyes for many years. If archetypes are playing themselves out, the cast for this universal play of the ages would encompass many different characters and a number of different scenarios. What may be happening? It may be very possible that darkness has simply set the stage for the light. The setting of the stage happens in a way that is similar to what happens in a movie theater. In a theater, just before the movie begins, the lights are all dimmed. After the darkness has filled the entire theater, suddenly, the movie starts and the actual moving pictures of light are enhanced and made manifest by the darkness.

How does this illustration apply to a musical drama unfolding on this planet? The musical theater of the world has grown dark. For many years the musical villains have set the stage by supplying the darkness. Eventually the heroes appear. The positive and negative are both necessary to reveal the truth. The light and darkness that are being projected in society are both imperative in order that the picture on the screen of reality can be observed. There are many different types of villains, such as were mentioned earlier.

In archetypal structures, there are often different types of villains. Some are obviously evil and others deceptively appear as good guys. They have been allowed to express their various degrees of darkness over extended periods of time. They become the obstacle that the hero has to overcome in order to obtain ultimate triumph. Many times villains are depicted as having stolen some valuable item to use in some perverted way. The hero has to take it back away from them.

The idea of being elevated to a higher level, by overcoming a musical structure is demonstrated by the musical scale as well. The death of the old scale is the birth of a new octave. Each new octave has to overcome the structure of the old scale. When it does, it is at an elevated position. The old scale has to be transcended in order to reach the higher octave.

If it is true that there are disharmonious musical villains at work in the world today, just as there were in ancient times, then it would make sense that they have musical weapons they are using against the unsuspecting masses. They would be using very covert methods to undermine the harmony of the world, while at the same time appearing good on the surface. What is the definition of the word "noise" in the dictionary? It is, "To assail with loud noise. To press with constant repetition" At this point, let's take a look at some of the more questionable traits of much of modern pop music to see if it fits the description of "noise".

Chapter 6

Questionable Traits Of Modern Music

In recent years a great controversy has arisen over what the proper tuning should be for music. There are two main schools of thought about this topic. One group says that the current concert pitch of 440 hertz is perfectly fine. Another group says that 440 hertz tuning is wrong and that standard concert pitch should be 432 hertz instead.

Those who hold to the 440 hertz tuning standard, are convinced it is adequate. Furthermore, they say that 432 hertz tuning sounds alright in one scale, but as it is played in other scales, it isn't as harmonious. The advocates of 440 hertz tuning, point to various groups of conspiracy theorists in the 432 hertz camp.They view some of the claims cited by the 432 hertz advocates as being ridiculous. For instance, some of the 432 advocates claim that standard concert pitch was changed by former Nazis from 432 to 440 in 1955. They claim that the 440 hertz tuning is being used to dumb humanity down so that they can be easily controlled. The advocates for 440 hertz tuning say there is no proof for this. Therefore, they dismiss the idea of using 432 hertz tuning entirely.

Advocates for 432 hertz tuning cite the fact that the frequencies of the 432 hertz scale match up better with the fundamental numbers of the universe. Advocates of 440 hertz tuning answer by saying that it doesn't matter what frequency you start a music scale on because numbers are arbitrary. There are numerous conspiracy claims that won't be covered in this book. Instead, let's take a look at what we do know about the number 432 from science and history. Here are a few facts to consider about the number 432.

One thing we do know is that the original Stradivarius violins, hand crafted by Antonio Stradivari were created to be tuned to 432 hertz. Stradivari dedicated his life to the perfecting of this violin. His Stradivarius violins are considered the finest ever made in standards of form, sound, and beauty. Why, in the crafting of an instrument of such perfection did he decide to tune it at 432 hertz? A man as brilliant and reasonable as what he was, had to have had a legitimate and scientific purpose for doing this.

The Fibonacci golden ratio, a mathematical pattern found in nature, was incorporated into the Stradivarius violin. Niccolo Paganini, one of the most legendary violinists of all time is known to have owned one of these 432 hertz tuned instruments. What can be learned from this? If nothing else, It would certainly appear that there is nothing wrong with creating an instrument made to be played in this tuning. Also, there may be some benefit to playing an instrument in 432 hertz.

Italian composer Giuseppe Verdi fought diligently to have the standard concert pitch set at 432 hertz in Italy. At some point, the Italian government granted him his request. It has also been claimed by a number of researchers that Bach, Beethoven, and Mozart each had some of their compositions played in Verdi (432 hertz) tuning.

In the time of Beethoven (1770-1827) there was a renowned acoustic scientist named Ernst Chladni (1756-1827). He is famous for his Chladni cymatics plates. He placed sand on thin, metal discs, and vibrated the sand on the plates with specific music frequencies. The sounds would produce geometric cymatic patterns in the sand on the plates.

Chladni spent many years studying the patterns that sound patterns produced in the sand on the plates. He knew that some sounds produced nearly perfect geometric forms in the sand and other frequency patterns produced deformed patterns. He published a textbook on the theory of music which explicitly defines the note "C"- 256 hertz as standard "scientific" or physical pitch for music. This tuning is the same as "A"-432.

Joseph Sauver, (1653-1716) who was called "the father of acoustics" was the first to state the fact that C= 256 was the most proper tuning. Sauver was also a contemporary of Bach. It is highly likely that Bach was familiar with Sauver's ideas.

Mozart (1756-1791) was born the same year as Ernst Chladni, and was born only three years after Joseph Sauver. Chladni and Sauver were two of the greatest acoustic scientists of Mozart's time. Both of these scientists stated that 256=C (432 hertz =A) was scientific musical pitch. Some researchers have stated that Mozart tuned precisely at 256=C. If so, this would make sense as he would have been following the best scientific knowledge of his day.

In moving this study to the current time frame, researchers are finding amazing things about the 432 hertz frequency. Jamie Buturff is a mechanical engineer. He has done an ample amount of research on the 432 hertz tone. Here are some interesting facts in his own words.

"The 432 hertz (scale) touches the full 12 scale octave overtones of all music in creation, whereas 440 hertz only touches 8 overtones, leaving out an entire section of the complete musical resonance of the universe. There is nothing harmonious either biologically or cosmically about the 440 hertz tone."

Buturff spoke of what shape the pure 432 hertz tone makes through, or on a cymatics instrument. "The pure 432 hertz sound makes the triangle shape of the trion ray. It is the smallest platonic solid that represents a single pulse of light in 3-D. This three sided shape tessellates to create the rest of the platonic solids. This shows that the 432 is in acoustical and structural harmony with the pulsations of light as it travels." It is interesting that 432 squared is very close to being the speed of light.

Through using math, acousticians have found that all of the basic principles of geometry, the golden ratio, and all of the platonic solids are in resonance with a scientific pitch of C=256 (or A=432). When officials raised the standard concert pitch to 440 hertz in 1955, music performed in concert halls around the world departed from being in resonance with the platonic solids, and universal structures. There is a very obscure archetype being acted out in the world through this action. The advocates of 432 hertz tuning imply that history is repeating itself due to the fact that one group has brought in a discrepancy, which has caused musical performances around the world to be out of tune with universal harmony.

In regards to how the scientific pitch of C= 256 is in harmony with the principles of geometry, take the pentagon shape for example. It exhibits the PHI ratio. This shape is also used to symbolize the structure of the human body. The pentagon gives us angles of 144, 108, 72, and 36 degrees. If one were to start at 36 degrees and continue to double following this geometric pattern, part of the sequence would be 432.

Buturff spoke of the great platonic year, as studied by Greek philosophers and how the grand cycle relates to the number 432. "It takes 25,920 years for the precession of the equinoxes. That is one complete cycle through all 12 signs of the zodiac. Today we are leaving the age of Pisces and entering the age of Aquarius. So there are 12 (ages of 2160 years) in one 25,920 year cycle.

If you multiply 432x60, you get 25,920. This is important because 60 is the base measurement of how we count time, 60 seconds to a minute, 60 minutes to an hour. The precession of the equinoxes and the 432 are literally revealing the timing of the pulse of life."

It is interesting to discover that the number 432 is connected to the timing of the pulse of life, in the universe and in the human body. The optimal and most healthy rate for a human heart to beat is 60 times a minute. That's 43,200 times every 12 hours, or 86,400 times in 24 hours. When the number 440 is used, it doesn't harmonize with any of the universal math, it's disharmonious.

If an instrument is tuned to Pythagorean tuning (also known as 432 hertz tuning) here is the list of what frequencies the notes of the scale should be tuned in.

do-256-C
re-288-D
mi-324-E
fa-344-F
sol-384-G
la-432-A
ti-486-B

It is interesting that all of these numbers can be found on the Stanford University list of the most harmonic numbers. This is not so with the numbers from the 440 tuned scale.

If you have been paying careful attention to what you are reading you may have noticed something. It would appear that once again an ancient archetype is playing itself out in the current time period. Think back to some of the most ancient information we know of. In sacred writings we hear stories of there being a place of perfect harmony. The ancient idea is that there were those types of beings who became disharmonious and brought in dissonance.That dissonance was a disharmony. The disharmony being spoken of in this context, is a spiritual disharmony. This is very subtle, but if you look at modern music, and the way that it has brought in a slight variation of tone which is not natural, you can see that it is disharmonious with creation.

While this may not be a big deal to many people, it may be highly symbolic of something that has taken place at a deeper level. Sometimes a slight ripple on the surface of the sea of sound may be indicative of a large movement that has taken place in the unseen depths. What we see played out in this world of physical matter, may be a distant, and barely detectable echo of a prior, larger, disharmony that took place in a higher dimension of a different kind.

There are many groups and organizations who are trying to get standard concert pitch changed back to 432 hertz tuning. Then, there are other groups and individuals who are prone to mocking those who are trying to do this. It's as if a mini-war has erupted over tones. One only needs to do a little research to witness the first hand battle between these two schools of thought. Who would have thought it? A modern day battle between what is seen as harmony and disharmony.

In ancient times, and even in the days of great composers like Mozart, there was an understanding that music is an expression of the hidden workings of the heavens. Music is a reflection of the laws of the universe. There was this idea that the hidden laws of nature and the universe should not be countered with musical tones whose math was out of harmony or synchronicity with them. Realistically ask yourself, does it make sense logically or mathematically to play 440 hertz scales when they are clearly out of tune with the mathematical principles of the universe?

Some modern musicians, who now recognize that their albums shouldn't have been recorded in 440 hertz tuning, are having their sounds transposed over into 432 hertz tuning. Their thought is that they can keep all of their old songs the same and if they simply transpose it over into 432 hertz, everything will just be fine. While this is a step in the right direction, it's not going to be the cure. This is because there are other problems that go beyond just what tuning the songs are being played in. Read on to find out what they are.

Chapter 7

The Origins Of American Music

There are other factors to consider about a lot of modern music. We've already learned that a lot of the music played over the last number of decades, would most likely never pass the standards required for music by ancient cultures, simply due to its tuning. What about its percussion instruments and the rhythms that are used? Let's examine this issue a bit deeper.

Actually when popular music first came to the United States in the 1950s and 1960s it was met by a storm of national protest. This was mainly because of its beat and because of all the ridiculous and crazy things teenagers did when they heard it. Why did so many people protest this form of music that had come to America? Why did so many people get upset over rhythm?

In order to more closely examine this, let's look at the background which preceded the arrival of backbeat music in the United States. In America, there were at least two major categories of music. One of them was sacred music. This music, researchers claim, could be traced from Jewish synagogues, on through Byzantine and Gregorian chant, into classical music, and then on to sacred music.

The other stream of music had its origins in West Africa in the religion of Vodun, better known as Voodoo. Music from the Vodun religion made its way to New Orleans with the slaves that came to the United

States from the Caribbean. Eventually voodoo influenced music found its way into the brothels of New Orleans, where elements of it became embodied in jazz music. Jazz music made its way up the Mississippi River to Chicago where it further morphed into rhythm and blues music. From there it made its way into rock and roll music.

Rock and roll is categorized by its syncopated rhythms, or backbeat which breaks the normal rhythms of music as they had been known to musical masters such as Bach, Beethoven, Mozart, and many other musical geniuses. One of the main rituals in the Vodun religion is to play various syncopated drum beats through which participants in the ritual call upon spirits to come and enter their bodies. The participants in the ritual are said to exhibit strange behaviors upon becoming possessed.

So, is it really a mystery as to why thousands of religious United States citizens protested the arrival of backbeat music and why civic leaders demanded that it be banned? Parents didn't like the effect it was having on their children or on society in general. People were rioting and acting crazy under its influence. What were people supposed to think of it? Entire communities held huge record burnings. They believed they had legitimate and intelligent reasons for protesting. There were most likely many intelligent people involved in the protests. They were simply trying to protect their children and their country.

However, the way that the beatnecks viewed the protestors was as ignorant fanatics. They were seen as dull and ignorant people who were backwards, stupid and boring. They were labeled as "squares". There were probably some protestors who were actually quite ignorant. They probably had no idea what they were even protesting, they were just doing what they were told to do. However, the IQs of the protestors was not the issue. It was the music. The music is what people failed to look into.

Let's take the whole backbeat music issue out of the realm of looking at it from a religious and historical perspective for just a moment, and look at it from a physical and scientific perspective to see what we can find.

Chapter 8

<hr>

A Deeper Look Into The Backbeat

An easy way to define a backbeat is simply with the word "syncopation". Let's look to New Webster's Home and Office Dictionary for the definition of "syncopation." Here is the definition. "To modify a piece of music by DISPLACING normal accents to create rhythmic CONTRADICTION."

Let's also look up another definition of the word "syncopation" from the Macmillan Dictionary. "A metric pattern created by stressing one or more NORMALLY UNACCENTED beats in a measure."

So, very simply put, what syncopation is, is an ABNORMAL set of beats. Normal accents are changed to ones which create rhythmic CONTRADICTION.

How would we know what a normal beat is? Do we have any examples of a proper beat? Is there something natural? Let's take a look at the human heartbeat. The human heart has a regular beat pattern, during which, blood is pumped through its four chambers and into the body. The main beat is called the "systolic" This takes place as blood is pumped from the left ventricle, out into the aorta and into the body. If we are to speak in musical terms about this process, this event occurs on the "first beat".

The secondary beat in the heart is known as the "diastolic" and occurs as blood is pumped from the right ventricle to the lungs. This is so that the blood can be replenished with fresh oxygen. If this is to be spoken of in musical terms, this occurs on the third beat.

Harmonious, well timed, and structured music emphasizes the first and third beats in a set pattern of rhythm, when the meter is in 4/4 timing. This is a natural biological pattern. The accented rhythm of a large majority of modern music is on the second and fourth beats. For this reason it is not in tandem nor in synchronization with the beat of the human heart.

Most modern music is played within normal pulse speed. Because of this, it has an off balanced beat pattern that will more directly be at odds with the heart beat. Due to the fact that most modern music is in similar time with the human pulse while at the same time it emphasizes an abnormal beat pattern, a mental and emotional tension is produced. This causes the blood pressure to rise.

In normal music, the first beat is a little bit louder and the third beat is a bit more subtle. In most modern pop music, the beat is equally strong on beats two and four. This is in direct contradiction to the natural universal beat of the heart. This is the reason it raises blood pressure.

It has been verified by medical studies that classical music lowers blood pressure and heart rate. Faster music with a heavier beat raises blood pressure. This was reported by the International Journal of Research in Medical Sciences. This is an open access international medical journal.

Let's do a brief summary of the main points we have covered in examining two of the elements of modern music. These two elements being tuning and rhythm. It is interesting to note, that the 432 mathematical tone has been shown to demonstrate a correspondence with the pulse of life, while the 440 hertz tone doesn't. Most modern music is recorded in 440 hertz tuning which puts it out of tune with the natural pulse of life shown in the universe. Secondly, a large majority of music heard on radio stations today contains back beat rhythms which have been shown to be just the opposite of the pulse of human life at the core of our physical being.

Someone may ask, well, if playing music in 440 hertz to a backbeat is somehow harmful, then why isn't everyone dead by now? This has been going on for decades, and some of the performers of that kind of music live super healthy, and into old age. Aren't there people who have listened to this type of music their whole lives who are living longer than ever? This may be true for some people on a physical level. However, what about the moral health of the nations of the world? What about the spiritual health of a people in any given culture? What about well defined and strong sexual gender characteristics? What has happened in these and other areas since more of this type of music has been listened to in the last century or more?

I want you to change your focus for a moment. We aren't necessarily referring to physical health with what has been being discussed. There may be something far more interesting and dangerous than that going on. Nobody is saying that these subtle musical problems are doing a tremendous amount of damage all at once. The effect may be gradual and we may not be seeing the full extent of the damage it has done yet.

Remember the ancient texts that speak of a place where highly elevated musical beings once lived together in perfect harmony? There were a number of super advanced musical beings in this harmonic world and eventually, some of them brought in a general dissonance. They brought disharmony to their world. If that scenario were to play itself out again on this planet, it would bring disharmony to many areas of life other than just the area of music. However, since the topic of this book is music, and we are speaking of how reflections of this ancient disharmony may show up in a very subtle way in today's music, let's say this. If perchance, it were to be mirrored in modern music, then wouldn't that scenario most likely require skilled musical people with extraordinary talent departing from the general rules and bringing in disharmony? Are the disharmonic factors we see in the current world of music just ripples to the surface, the echoes and reflection of an event from long ago? Once again, you decide. These are all just questions for you to consider.

In our study, let's move on now from this brief look at how music played in 440 hertz tuning to the timing of a backbeat affects the human heart, and let's see what kind of effect it has on plants.

Chapter 9

Plant Biology and Music

The music study done in 1973 by researcher Dorothy Retallack at the Colorado Women's College in Denver may shed light on the topic of modern music and its effect on biological plant life.

Retallack did experiments studying the relationship that music had on plants. This involved seeing what kind of effect different types of music would have on plants. She began her experiments by using a single tone. In the experiment, there were three chambers. In the first chamber she played a non-ceasing tone for eight hours straight. In the second chamber she played the tone off and on for only three hours at a time. In the third chamber, there was no tone at all.

The plants in the first chamber which were continuously subjected to the tone, died within 14 days. The plants in the second chamber grew rapidly and were vibrantly healthy. The plant in the second chamber did better than the plant in the chamber which had no sound at all.

In one of the experiments, Retallack put fresh plants into two chambers. Rock music was played in one of the chambers, and softer, calm music was played in the other chamber. The amount of time the music was played in each one of the chambers was three hours.

By the fifth day of the experiment significant changes were discovered. In the chambers with the more soothing music, the plants were growing healthy, and their stems were starting to bend toward the speakers. In the chamber playing the rock music, half of the plants had small leaves and had grown gangly. The other plants in the chamber where rock music was playing were stunted in their growth.

After two weeks had passed, the plants that were subjected to soothing music were equal in size. They were green, lush, and were leaning 15 to 20 degrees towards the speaker. Plants in the chamber playing hard rock music had grown extremely tall and were drooping. The blooms had faded and the stems were bending away from the speaker.

By day 16, the plants that were in the chambers playing rock music were in the last stages of dying. In the other chamber, the plants were abundant and lush. Basically, in all of the experiments that were done, the plants that were subjected to Classical music, or softer music, did much better.

Why was this? What conclusions do you come to from this simple experiment? Do these types of results show up just in botany life, or do we see results like these in other areas as well? Let's see what sound can do to water.

Chapter 10

The Effect of Sound on Water

There are videos on line which show sound forming geometrical patterns on the surface of water. Scientists have known what sound can do to water for many decades. In the early 2000s, a Japanese man by the name of Dr. Emato published a book called, "Messages From Water". In his book, he claims to have proven that classical music has a good effect on water, while much of rock music doesn't.

In his experiments, researchers would place bottles of water in between speakers. The distilled water in the bottles would be blasted with music. After the water was permeated with sound, it would be frozen. In its frozen state, the water would be sliced into thin slices and then Dr. Emato would look at the ice crystals in the frozen slice of water to see what shape they were. Emato reported that water subjected to Beethoven's "Pastoral Symphony" produced ice crystals that were well formed and beautiful. He stated that when Mozart's 40th symphony was played to water, the ice crystals that resulted were elegant.

In fact, nearly any classical music the water was subjected to was said to have produced beautifully mathematically patterned ice crystals. Not so, with heavy metal music. That type of music produced ugly and deformed looking ice crystals.

Another amazing effect that demonstrates the amazing effect of sound on water is called sonoluminescence. Sonoluminescence is the emission of light from imploding bubbles in water when excited by sound. It occurs when a soundwave of sufficient intensity induces a gaseous cavity within water to collapse quickly, emitting a burst of light.

Chapter 11

The Effect of Sound Upon Matter

Cymatics is the study of how sound vibrations can affect matter. If a thin metal disc has random grains of sand placed on it, and then that disc is made to vibrate by music notes or sound frequencies, the sand setting upon the disc will become arranged into geometrical patterns.

The patterns will vary according to what musical pitch is vibrating it. When notes from the 432 hertz scale are sent through the instrument, and the disc is made to vibrate accordingly, the sand will begin to become formed into perfect geometrical shapes. In some cases, certain vibrations or frequencies will begin forming botanical shapes, geometrical shapes, floral shapes, and even the shapes of living creatures such as dragonflies.

What is really interesting, is that it has been studied and when Pythagorean tuning notes are used, the sand will arrange itself into perfectly defined geometrical shapes. The frequencies from the 440 hertz scale will also arrange itself into shapes, but ones which are not as clearly and precisely arranged. There can be slight deformities in such cases.

It has been discovered that various stars and planetary bodies are all sending out certain frequencies. When these frequencies are run through a cymatics instrument, it is revealed that the star frequencies create patterns as well. We know that the sun, which is a star, emits stellar energies which affect plants and all life on Earth. What about all of the other suns shining through the universe whose rays strike our planet? What kind of effect do they have on our plants, and therefore on the food we eat? We sometimes forget that when we absorb the nutritional energy from food, we are absorbing the stellar energy from which the plant received its nourishment. The human body functions by stellar energy.

In various places around the world, various patterns have been found inscribed in sacred places that until now, were not recognized as being cymatic patterns. It would appear as if, sometime in the ancient past, sages knew the frequencies which were beneficial to the human race, and which ones were detrimental. Various places, such as Solomon's temple are believed to have been designed in such a way to produce the best possible acoustics.

When one realizes that the ancients seem to have recognized that there were beneficial and detrimental frequencies, the question arises, where did they get this knowledge? They seemed to understand this much better than we do today. It becomes easier to understand why ancient cultures had stricter guidelines and higher standards they held their music to. Think back to the idea which states that the very source of the battle we face today, has its origins in the battle between harmonious and disharmonious musical super beings. The effect of beneficial and detrimental vibrational frequencies on the planet is being understood to a greater extent every day.

Chapter 12

The Effect of Music On Animals

Various types of music affect animals as well. The Journal of Veterinary Behavior reports that researchers at Colorado State University have proven this fact.

In one experiment, researchers played classical music, an altered style of classical music, and heavy metal music for dogs. When different types of classical music were played, the dogs slept more than what they did with no music. This indicates that they were more relaxed.

The dogs were reported to have had the opposite reaction to heavy metal music. While they were listening to heavy metal music, they had increased body shaking which showed that their stress levels increased.

It was also found that cows produced more milk when listening to music like, "Bridge Over Troubled Water" or Beethoven's "Pastoral Symphony". Elephants have even been filmed swaying their tails to violin music. These studies are consistent with research done on human beings. Softer music reduces agitation, promotes sleep, improves mood, and lowers stress and anxiety.

What could possibly be the common factor wherein all of these various areas of life seem to be affected by music? There are some who believe that it may have something to do with the Earth's magnetic field. Human beings, plants, and animals are all interfaced, infused and integrated directly into the Earth's magnetic currents.

Human beings have energy fields and the Earth itself has an energy field.This energy comes from outer space. Both the Earth's magnetic field and the magnetic field of our bodies operate by the same energy from space. This energy field has been photographed many times surrounding the human body. We know it as an aura. It can be seen surrounding plants and animals as well. When people, plants, or animals die, the energy field disappears. It has been discovered that the nutrition which we receive through our food actually comes from outer space. The plants get their energy directly from space and then we consume the plants. The plants also pull nutrients up from the ground where stellar energy has been stored in minerals. There are some who have speculated that when we take vitamins and minerals all we are really doing is strengthening those magnetic poles in our bodies. Our bodies then begin pulling down and drawing more of those particular energies from space and into our bodies. Thus, our bodies are then brought back into equilibrium and perfect balance with the Earth's magnetic field. Some have theorized that one day it will be discovered that we can bypass food as an agent for nutrition and get our nutrition directly from the energies of space. What do you think?

The Greek philosopher Plato stated that within the flow of this magnetism there are times of fertility and times of sterility. He reported that during times of magnetic fertility, there are more artists and musicians. During times of magnetic sterility, there is a lack of creativity. Artists and musicians, as well as other people are at times responding to the tidal forces of magnetic currents. There are times of magnetic nourishment and times of magnetic deprivation. People are said to be more healthy during times of magnetic nourishment, and are sick more often when magnetism is weak.

The movements of magnetic fields are thought to be apparent in nature as well. Just before an earthquake takes place, animals move away from areas of danger. Birds may leave the area entirely. It is thought that they do this because of their close connection to the Earth's magnetic field. They can instinctively sense a change in the field. It was observed in Japan that seconds before an earthquake, magnets become demagnetized. Subtle changes take place in the atmosphere. Sometimes there is a peculiar stillness before an earthquake. These are subtle hints of changes within the Earth's magnetic field.

Many sages have observed through the years that there seems to be a connection between the sins of man and the revolt of the elements. Plato stated that when the people of Atlantis became increasingly immoral, suddenly there was an upheaval of nature and the entire continent was destroyed in a night. Some people believe that when people sin, it weakens the magnetic fields of their bodies and eventually of the Earth itself. Religious rules that have come down to us through the centuries may be showing us how to keep our magnetic fields strong as well as the fields of the Earth. There may be no apparent consequences for breaking the rules for years, and then suddenly there is destruction. This often comes in the form of sicknesses, plagues, and natural disasters. Dr. Walter Kilner (1847-1920) was a British physician who was one of the first to study the human aura and its changes in appearance during sickness and health. It has been found that before any sickness appears in the physical body, it can first be detected in the body's aura. Anton Mesmer was another scientist known world wide for his studies on magnetism.

There are many different types of events that are thought to be somehow related to the magnetic field. Here is a different way of looking at magnetic fields. Thomas Edison had a neighbor that passed away. Edison noticed that at the very moment of his neighbor's death, a dog down the street began howling as if he had sensed a change in the Earth's magnetic field due to the death of the person. Animals are very intune with the magnetic field. Perhaps human beings are as well. Albert Einstein talked about this connection. He said, "We (humans) are slowed down sound and light waves, a walking bundle of frequencies tuned into the cosmos". In other words. We are engrafted right into the tidal forces and powers of space. We are constantly interacting with these laws whether we realize it or not. We are believed to have a direct connection with the magnetic field of the Earth. In fact, even our thoughts are believed to have a connection to magnetism. Brain cells contain microscopic particles of magnetite, which are magnetic iron oxide.

Interestingly, academic journals report that subatomic particles are harmonic in nature. The structure of atoms contains ratios and numbers which demonstrate the harmonic principles of music. Human beings are composed of atoms. This is interesting because it would seem to indicate that there is a music of the spheres within. We know that the solar system is exhibiting musical ratios through the orbit of the planets. We also know that the way electrons orbit within atoms is similar to the way planets orbit the sun. So it really is not all that surprising that there would be a music of the spheres within.

Earlier in the book there was a discussion on archetypes. Archetypes are thought by some to be patterns of energy that play themselves out over and over. There are some who believe that archetypical energy patterns are stored within the Earth's magnetic field. How could they be stored? Perhaps they get stored within the atmosphere the same way that other types of energy waves get stored in the atmosphere. Here is an example. During the Vietnam War in the 1960s, an American ship out on the ocean began to pick up a very strange radio transmission. Suddenly, sailors on the ship began to hear both Japanese and American fighter pilots from World War Two on their radio. Those broadcasts were electromagnetic waves, and they had been floating around out over the ocean in that area for decades. Due to some kind of condition on that particular day the radio waves were refracted back down into the atmosphere and were picked up by the ship's radio even though it was decades later. Perhaps archetypical energy patterns are stored in the atmosphere in a similar manner.

Earth's magnetic field was made to be in perfect equilibrium, order, and balance. Nature is always correcting itself. If musicians are constantly pouring their non Pythagorean tunings, and their rhythms which are contrary to the human heartbeat into the atmosphere all over the world, what problems may they be causing? Or, is it as they say, "It's no problem. It's perfectly fine. We're just having fun. We all love one another." Do they really? Remember earlier in the book the finding of Dr. Emato was discussed. It was found that words have a profound effect on water. Good words produce orderly shapes in ice crystals. Evil words of hate produce disorderly and disharmonious ice crystals. Dr. Hans Jenny, as well as many others, have demonstrated that dissonant tones produce disharmonious forms on a cymatics instrument. Many performers are going all over the world spewing hateful words and dissonant tones into the air and they are leading us to believe that this is perfectly alright just because they're making good money and having fun? Despite the fact that many are doing this, something is still working according to an overall plan to bring things to a higher level. Somehow all of this is necessary in the musical chemistry of the ages.

There are more and more studies being done on how the human mind is directly connected and infused into the Earth's magnetic field. The human aura is said to change according to a person's mood, and the aura is directly connected to the Earth's magnetic field. Some studies seem to indicate the magnetic field can be affected by the human mind, behavior, and conduct. If one is to keep this in mind, then it may make more sense to you why the sacred scriptures tell us to love our neighbors and follow divine law. We are told to do unto others as we'd have them do unto us. To not do so may be to affect the Earth's magnetic field in an adverse way.

This planet is made to survive. On its own, it purifies the water, cleans the air, gets rid of pestilence, and does many things. Many of the ills of the human body heal on their own. The human body is made to survive and everything around you is designed to go on perpetually. It's the human race that has gotten out of harmony. Nearly everything else works like clockwork, most of the time. The entire universe is orderly, and nature is orderly. The universe is showing us the music of the spheres. The natural patterns of planet Earth and the natural processes are running at least somewhat parallel to the universal forces. Human beings should too. The failure to do so brings problems.

The invisible lines of the magnetic field travel in a closed, continuous loop, flowing into the Earth at the north magnetic pole and out at the south magnetic pole. The solar wind compresses the field's shape on the Earth's sun facing side, and stretches it into a long tail on the night-facing side. Humans, animals, and plants all have magnetic fields, and we are electrical. This is the reason you have the power to give someone else an electrical shock. This is why you can rub a balloon in your hair and stick it to the ceiling. What goes on in the field affects us directly or indirectly.

Magnetic currents have tidal forces. There are ebbs and flows. Thomas Aquinas wrote that the magnetic fields of human bodies are subject to these magnetic tides. Albertus Magnus stated that the human mind has fluids in it that are subject to magnetism. It's important to think the right types of thoughts and have the right actions. These right actions include creating the right type of harmonious music.

Each piece of music creates a magnetic field. Neurologists and psychologists have informed us that certain styles of music are damaging. Certain types of music do damage to the human body. Many radio stations and performers are tearing down magnetic fields through wrong attitudes, decadent lifestyles, promoting drug use, alcoholism, lyrics of hate,violence, racism and prejudice. Meanwhile the music they play reflects this mental atmosphere. It further brings about the decline of civilization.

Over the decades there have been a large number of musicians who have lived decadent lives. They have unleashed their noise upon the masses. They have used tunings and rhythms out of tune with the natural processes of the Earth and universe. Many of the subjects they have chosen to sing about have often been foolish,perverse and demoralizing. The lifestyles they have lived and the mindsets they have chosen may have been an attack on the magnetic fields of the Earth and human body.

They've made fun of spiritual things. They say, "get off our backs, we're just having a good time. We're not hurting anyone." Are they sure? Despite this fact, they are still loved. Here is one question though. With all the love coming their way isn't it time for musicians to change their minds, be forgiven for anything wrong they've done, and accept the call and responsibility to do as much good for as many people as they possibly can with their talents? Isn't it time to obey divine and universal laws and morals?

Here's a suggestion for musicians and artists. Stop rolling your eyes at people who are trying to bring back spiritual and moral law. Nobody is going to be perfect overnight, but what if musicians and songwriters at least made an attempt to take steps in the right direction? That's not to say many steps haven't already been taken. Let's turn the notch up on our efforts! We can do better. Most of us have been involved in at least some of these mistakes at some point in our lives. We are all guilty. Aren't you tired of it? Don't you want to do right and move into the fantastic potential of music used correctly? What if we discovered how to strengthen the Earth's magnetic field with music, rather than weaken it?

Chapter 13

Facing The Music

There is really no way around the fact that some elements in modern music aren't ideal. This fact needs to be faced rather than ignored if things are ever going to improve with the artform. A person can look into a mirror and not like what they see, the mirror isn't lying to you. What you see, is what you see. There is evidence which has surfaced through many different studies that show us we should be trying to improve music. We should be looking into ways as to how to retain what is good in music while trying at the same time to eliminate the bad.

Some of the readers of this book may not like the results of some of these studies, but they are what they are. They show what they show. Some may try to deny them. The question is, why? Why not take this information and try to do something about it? One of the problems is that many of the proponents of modern music close their eyes to all of these facts. They have a tendency to ignore any information that would appear to be contrary to what they are doing.

They also have a tendency to produce their own studies which aren't really being honest. For example, rather than facing the fact that some modern music increases blood pressure, they will change the wording and present it in such a way as if it's something positive. They may in such a case say something like, It's been proven that our music increases blood flow, rather than to just simply admit that it raises blood pressure.

The truth is not prejudiced. What is true is true. If you play harmonious frequencies and rhythms, you will get harmony and equilibrium. If you play dissonant frequencies and rhythms, you'll get dissonance. It's as simple as that. It's universal law. Adherence to the set rules of nature will produce the same results whether you are a Christian, a Jew, a Muslim, a Pagan, an Atheist, an Agnostic, or whatever persuasion or beliefs you may be of.

The laws of music don't care if you're red, yellow, black, or white. If you break the musical laws, you'll get dissonance. If you work with the natural laws of music, you'll get harmony. There are some real problems with a lot of this era's music. Some of it is outright toxic. Solving these problems requires a balanced approach. It calls for those who will deal with the problems with a spiritual and rational mind. One thing that can be clearly noticed in the modern world, is that there are many people in country music and much of the so called "gospel" music worlds that somehow have gotten the idea that their particular brand of music is the chosen medium for scriptural messages. How is this? Country and contemporary "gospel" music in the current time frame contains all of the same dissonant properties as the harder music. Most of it uses the same backbeats, distorted instruments, lack of variation, non Pythagorean tunings, and other bad elements that the other music uses.

No matter what type of modern music is played, there's bound to be at least some good in it, just as there are a few good nutrients in absolute junk food. Does that mean that junk food is good? Even in the worst sugary lemonade there's bound to be a small amount of vitamin C. There is a tendency in all musicians to overlook the shortcomings of their music and then concentrate on all the good elements in what they are doing. There's bound to be a few antioxidants in the worst sugary candy bar.

This time period requires a lot of musical forgiveness. People have been confused. Until recently, there hasn't been a lot of information available to the public on this topic. Most people that pick up a musical instrument probably have at least some good intentions. We all make mistakes, and we can all move on from here trying to make things better. If you find that you've made mistakes, try to do better. Try to eliminate the mistakes. Study great composers like Bach and Beethoven. See what their inspirations and philosophies of music were. When you find something good, try to emulate it.

As far as analyzing the good and bad in music, move forward with an inquiring mind. Everything has to be dealt with on a song by song basis. The same composer may on one day accidently write a dissonant piece of toxic music, while on the very next day the very same person may write a musical masterpiece that is divine, harmonious, and life-giving. If musicians make mistakes, be merciful, be forgiving, knowing that none of us are perfect. Be happy of the fact that we live in a free world where we have freedom of expression, and freedom of speech. They have been given the freedom to make mistakes, just like you have. Recognize the fact that they have made a musical mistake, and then move forward. You don't have to listen to them. They have no power over you that the simple pressing of a button to turn them off won't cure.

Over the years, one of the problems that seems to have cropped up in the world of music, is as follows. Let's say that at one point, a recording artist creates a very dissonant and toxic piece of music. They are then labeled as horrible by certain groups within society. That branch of society then writes them off entirely. They refuse to give these recording artists a second chance and they seem very eager to do this.

Then, when that same artist later uses their heavenly gift, and comes up with a divinely inspired masterpiece, certain sects of society proclaim that it's evil anyway. What they are then guilty of doing, is proclaiming a divinely inspired gift, and musical composition to be Satanic. This is a serious offense.

There is a story about John Sebastian Bach, sneaking into a church one night to play a pipe organ. Somebody came in and heard him playing.

This particular person, hearing Bach play, was amazed by the playing. The observer left the church and went out and told people that the Devil himself must have gotten into the church and was playing the organ.

This is a very typical attitude that seems to have stuck with religious society through the centuries. There are a number of religious people and groups who love to give the Prince of Darkness credit for being a fantastic musician. At the same time, they completely ignore the harmonic virtues of the very one they claim to be serving. They forget that in the scriptures it is The Universe Maker who is the progenitor of music, and not the dark lord. Celestial beings sang long before Cain.

Some people are just music haters to begin with. It seems as if it's because many of them have no musical ability themselves. Martin Luther had the following to say about such people; "A person who…. Does not regard music as a marvelous creation of God, must be a clodhopper indeed and does not deserve to be called human being; he should be permitted to hear nothing but the braying of asses and the grunting of hogs." Luther was also quoted as saying, "The Devil should not be allowed to keep all the best tunes for himself".

Problems within music do need to be brought to attention. They have to be brought into awareness in order to be corrected. What may actually work better than having a critical attitude is to try to encourage people towards musical idealism. Sometimes it may work best to try to lead by example. The problem with that is, we are all human beings who make mistakes. As long as we are in the human condition, we are going to have failures. So, the question of how much of an example we can actually be is questionable in the first place. However, this shouldn't keep people from shooting for perfection. While people are shooting for perfection, and are still making mistakes, then, I would suggest ample forgiveness from the critics. What many critics seem to expect is that the musicians would bury their talents.

In the 1950s and 1960s, there were those who tried to warn people about some of the problems that were surfacing with music. Science is beginning to prove that at least some of what they said was true.

There are some elements that actually do need to be corrected. Much of the artistic community will never admit that some of it needs to be corrected, even to this day.

Even though those who opposed modern music did have some legitimate points, they had some serious problems as well. Although some of the music did have some toxic elements within it, there were also some highly inspired masterpieces that were mixed in with them. The opposers of modern music seemed bound and determined to go on a witch hunt and demonize music. Evidently, it was easier to just be critical of everything. It was too much work for them to go through the music and separate the good from the bad in it.

Basically, it was pure laziness. There seemed to be a huge lack of true effort to diligently recognize the divine gifts in people who were making mistakes with what they were doing with music. There also seems to have been a real lack of love and concern for the musicians from the various groups that were criticizing them. There was also a monumental failure to try to instruct people in the correct way. There's got to be a right way to do it.

The religious factions who were being critical of the music, often pointed to the fact that Lucifer had musical instruments built right into him. However, what they never seemed to bring up, is the fact that, of course he did. He was an angel and angels are musical beings. Who's to say that all angels don't have musical instruments and abilities?

Before long, they had him pegged as being the song leader, and a singer in a prior heavenly world. What they never seemed to bring up however, is that it is the Creator who the ancient Hebrews considered to be the Master Musician of the Universe, and not the Evil One. Conveniently for them and their side of the argument, this fact was swept under the rug. This was, and is, a very strange situation. It is a situation in which pious and religious people are willingly ignorant concerning the musical attributes of the one they claim to be serving, while at the same time they continue to heap praise and recognition on The Adversary for all his skilled musical attributes and abilities.

There are many different compartments to a music composition, many different factors. All of the areas need to be considered in analyzing a piece of music. Someone may, at a certain point, compose a so-called music composition that really doesn't amount to much more than a toxic piece of noise. However, even if the music itself is disharmonious, there may be other parts of the song that are excellent. For instance, the lyrics may be very profound. In those cases, instead of criticizing the composition as a whole, wouldn't it be better to give them credit for the great lyrics, and then just tell them that the music itself needs work?

A word to the critics here. You have to remember that most people who are making mistakes with music have no idea that they are doing anything wrong. They didn't have bad intentions. They may have had selfish ones, but at the same time had good motives as well.

In one sense of the word, you can see why music was controlled by the state in some ancient cultures. However, it doesn't seem to be the right way. Why is this? Musicians need to be given the freedom to experiment. They have to be given the liberty to make mistakes. Most learning in many areas of life is accomplished through trial and error.

Some of the mistakes that have been made with music in the past may have needed to have been allowed so that they could be exposed and then the whole art form could move forward into better things. How do you know what light is unless darkness has been given the opportunity to express itself? Can you really be angry at the proponents of musical darkness when darkness is the necessary element that's needed in order that light can be made manifest?

We are aiming at the idea of musical idealism here, but musicians need to be cut some slack. Many of the musical instruments made these days have been designed to play in the wrong frequencies. Until these instruments are redesigned and manufactured there's nothing that can be done to play them in the correct frequencies. Many times when film-makers and other artists are putting projects together, all they have available to them is music played in inferior frequencies. That's why there needs to be grace towards artists. In the meantime, all that artists can do is just do the best they can with what they've got to work with. More companies should be encouraged to produce musical instruments that use the 432 hertz scale.

If two major things could be accomplished in the world of music, it would be epic. What are these two things? Number one, music artists should just be honest and admit that some of the music that they have presented to society is toxic and disharmonious. They should freely face the fact that some of it is a detriment to society. Then, they should take steps to try to correct it. It would take things to an entirely new and better level. They'd actually be happier in the long run.

Number two, if the music haters in the world would stop demonizing some of the music compositions that are actually divine, we would be far better off as a society. If they would do everything in their power to help musicians retain that which is good and give musicians credit for what is good in their music, we would be better off as a society. Have musicians made mistakes with their compositions? Yes, of course. Have they exhibited moments of divine genius through the gifts they've been given? The answer to this is yes too. There are a large number of people on this planet that need to stop hating music and do what they can to help those who are trying to make good music. They'd be much happier if they'd try that route. They need to stop throwing the musical baby out with the musical bath water.

Chapter 14

Understanding Musical Ideologies

When people have a dislike of modern music, we need a better understanding of what mindsets and beliefs they are coming from. We have to ask ourselves what has caused them to come to these conclusions. We have to consider their reasoning.

Modern musicians would have to admit that a lot of the music that people have listened to for the last few decades is dissonant when compared to a large amount of music from earlier times. Much of it literally qualifies more as noise than it does music, when put to the test of the standards for music found in ancient cultures. Much of it bears no resemblance to what people called "music" in places such as Greece during Neoplatonic times. This is simply the truth. Does this mean that the Greeks were always right about everything? By no means.

Much of modern mainstream music bears very little resemblance to much of the music of the ancient masters. There are also ideological differences. Let's narrow our focus here for just a moment. Let's look at an example of a musical ideology from the past that stands in stark contrast to a lot of the ideologies of musicians today. With an understanding of these older ideologies, perhaps it will be easier for modern musicians to see why some people have criticized their music.

To begin with, in many cultures chaos or disorder was seen as evil, and harmony and order was seen as good. The very origin of evil at that time, was, and is still believed to have found its genesis in those who brought disharmonic chaos to heaven. Although this topic was covered, at least partially earlier in the book, let's delve a bit deeper into the thoughts concerning it. The following is an example of a type of thinking which was prevalent during the Renaissance, in regards to harmony and disharmony. Let's investigate this philosophy a bit deeper here. By examining the thoughts of Jacob Boehme, we can come to a better understanding of Renaissance thought on the subject of music.

Jacob Boehme was an influential writer and personality in the late 1400s and early 1500s. He was a Lutheran who believed the writings of Martin Luther. He was a German philosophical mystic who had a profound influence on later movements such as idealism and Romanticism.

Jacob Boehme author and researcher of the late 1400s and early 1500s.

He believed that there were different types of angelic beings who dwelt in a perfect and orderly realm thousands of years ago. He was convinced that each of the different types of angels had their own unique types of songs. He compared the various styles of different types of angelic music to various strings on a single instrument.

In his way of thinking, each of these different groups of spiritual beings would sing. He compared each of seven different angelic singing groups to a string on a musical instrument. In a way that was similar to how various strings can be arranged into a chord and all can be sounded together to become one harmonious sound on a stringed instrument, so were all the various songs of all the different types of angels, according to Boehme.

He was of the opinion that if you were to take one of the groups of angels, of which there may be countless billions of them all singing powerful songs at once, and join their music to other large groups of spiritual beings singing, the singing would perfectly harmonize between the various groups. Their songs would all be completely different from one another, yet when all seven of these groups' songs came together, all the songs would become one song. The songs would fit together flawlessly.

Boehme said the details of this concept were divinely revealed to him. Some didn't believe him. Regardless, the concept gives a glimpse into how seriously they took the idea of well orchestrated and orderly music in his day. If an inquiring mind is to take this type of idea back to ancient Egyptian times and look for this type of idea there, one finds a strict and orderly concept of music. The ancient Egyptians had a musical note assigned to every hour of the day. They were meticulous in their representations of it. What was their inspiration for this type of thinking? Why did they believe music had to be so orderly? It was believed by many Egyptians that music was introduced to ancient Egypt by Hermes Trismegistus.

Boehme's writings were very influential during the Renaissance. He taught that all people on Earth were themselves musical instruments.

Everyone was playing either good or bad "music". Their very lives were thought to be the music they were playing. Everything they did gave off a "sound". In other words, the words they spoke, the actions they took, the lives they lived were the "sound" they were giving off. All of these areas of life combined together became the musical atmosphere they were creating. He believed and taught that the vibes they were making were either harmonious or disharmonious.

An illustration from a Jacob Boehme book from the Renaissance.
Notice the trumpet in the hand of the center figure.

He was of the opinion that you only needed to listen to a person talk for a while to be able to hear or understand what type of note they were sounding. As they lived out their lives, time would tell what type of instrument they were and who was playing them. What is meant by that?

Long ago, the human body was likened to a musical instrument. Among some people, the human spine was seen as a fretboard of a stringed instrument, the nerves that ran down the spine were seen as the strings running down the neck of the instrument. Their idea was, That human beings were being played by either a good spirit or a bad spirit. Not all religious people saw things that way, but those who followed Boehme did.

Furthermore, the ancient battle which once took place in a prior world between the good and bad spirits had come down to Earth and was being played out once more on this planet. Some were tuned into the Master Musical Conductor of the universe, and others were tuned into the disharmonious ones. It is unknown as to whether they saw this belief as a reality playing itself out physically, or if they saw this idea as a symbolic metaphor which helped them understand a spiritual reality.

Boehme's ideas may have stemmed back to the idea found in a number of religions. The idea of spiritual beings who were musical beings. Since he knew that at least some of these beings were musicians, and that these spiritual beings had an influence on humans, it was thought that human beings could be played like musical instruments by spiritual beings. People had free will. They could decide whether they wanted to be in harmony with spiritual laws or not. The type of harmony and disharmony spoken of in this context was something that went far beyond the idea of just audible harmony and disharmony.

Jacob Boehme believed that way back before there was a universe, there was a place where all of the polarities such as light and darkness, harmony and disharmony, good and evil, were all mixed together. He believed that these opposites, such as order and disorder, were engaged in mortal combat against each other. In short, he believed in a conflict of polarities. He was of the mindset that nothing can come into manifestation without its contrary equivalent. For example, you can't know what light is without darkness. You can't understand what union is without division. You have no knowledge of what harmony is without disharmony.

He taught that this conflict of polarities is what was necessary in order for good to be made manifest. In other words, nothing can be made plain without its opposite. Boehme maintained that before human or angelic time began, before there was either heaven or earth, there was a mixing of polarities in a place beyond human comprehension. In this incomprehensible place was order and disorder, harmony and dissonance, good and evil, light and darkness, and all polarities.

In this mysterious place of the unmanifested, the polarities were gathered into separateness. In other words, light separated itself from darkness. In this context, what he was referring to, was spiritual light being separated from spiritual darkness. Good attributes were separated from what would become bad attributes.

As this conflict of polarities continued, the spiritual light became more and more separated from spiritual darkness. Harmony separated from dissonance, order was separated from chaos, good was separated from evil, love was separated from hate.

Boehme maintained that at a certain point, there was a flash, and light merged out of the darkness. The manifested came forth out of the mysterious unmanifested realm. That which came into manifestation was called light. That which was unmanifested was thought of as the darkness. The light (manifested) came out of the darkness (the unmanifested). Light came out of darkness similar to the way a star is born. Harmony came out of disharmony.

According to Boehme's theological writings, when light came out of darkness, a whole world of spiritual light came into being. It was a world of perfect harmony, perfect order, and perfect balance. Boehme implied that the spiritual inhabitants of this world of light knew nothing but harmony, light, and perfection. According to Boehme, Lucifer was a high ranking "light being" who knew nothing but light and perfection. However, he wanted to know what his creator knew, Lucifer had only known good, he wanted to know both good and evil. He was in a world of light and harmony, but was interested in the opposites of light and harmony. It was as if he felt that his Maker had an unfair advantage over him by knowing both good and evil. The sum of what the spiritual beings in that world of light knew, was only good. So according to Boehme, Lucifer hatched a plan to take over by rebelling to bring in a state of both spiritual light and darkness, then he thought he would be like the Originator, knowing both good and evil.

Boehme wrote that there was once a place of light and harmony where there was no darkness. Notice the music notes above the head of the figure sitting on the celestial sphere.

Boehme implied that Lucifer had some kind of an inkling, that the Begetter had a certain knowledge he was keeping from the inhabitants of the world of pure light. In order for there to be a world of only good, it had to have been created out of some place that served as a reference point. There had to be a place which was its opposite. Boehme claimed that the beings of light had never experienced the wrath of their Originator. He contended that when a war broke out, it then incited the indignation of The Absolute, and the beings of light who lived in that perfect place had never seen anger exhibited. In other words, Lucifer and his disharmonious followers provoked their Designer to be moved to an act of wrath that had up until that point been an aspect of the Creator that was restrained from being exhibited in that world of perfect light and harmony. However, when Lucifer and his instigators put the whole kingdom of harmony into a war, it became necessary to do something about them.

According to Boehme, righteous anger was an aspect of their Maker that had previously been hidden from the light beings. In righteous anger he kicked Lucifer and his light beings out of that flawless world of light.

An etching by R. Pranker from the late 1700s depicting Lucifer
and his followers being cast out of the elevated place.

After that, said Boehme, a decision to make another perfect world was
implemented. This perfect world was planet Earth. At that time it was
paradise. Lucifer, who was now the Devil, had access to planet Earth.
He tricked the first woman Eve into thinking that her heavenly parent

was hiding godhood from her. Through her disobedient act, and by convincing her husband to disobey as well, a mixed world of both light and darkness was ushered in, and the whole world was thrown out of harmony.

So, according to Boehme's idea, we now live in a world of both spiritual harmony and dissonance. There has been an ongoing battle between good and evil on this planet. This battle shows up in many different areas in this world. The fact that Boehme uses musical language quite often in his descriptions, does not mean that he is describing something that is primarily some kind of a musical battle. However, when he is speaking of a spiritual battle between harmony and disharmony, he is using these descriptions metaphorically.

This world was intended to be a place of perfect order. It was supposed to operate in perfect harmony with the universe. Here is a question for you. When the music of human beings is examined, and it is found that it is out of accordance with the finer principles of mathematical perfection, is this a subtle reflection of disorder at a higher level? Can it be traced back to a time before the foundation of the world? This is another thought for you to mull over.

Boehme obviously took some of these ideas directly from sacred scripture. However, one will notice from reading his works that he seems to add in a bunch of detail. He says that the ideas he presented were a divine revelation. We find these themes in a number of writings. Whether or not you believe them, you are going to have to decide. Remember, these aren't new ideas. This is just a presentation of the ideas held by sages from the remote past. This is simply a report.

Boehme's thinking was quite well known and accepted by a large number of religious people in his day. For many hundreds of years, you'd hear prominent people speaking of the idea of harmony and dissonance.

For example, Emanuel Swedenborg was a Swedish theologian, scientist, philosopher, and mystic. He lived from 1688-1772. It was commonly reported that he began having visions of heaven and hell starting in 1744. He said that while visiting another world, he observed spiritual beings living in communities. He spoke of how important living in harmony was in that other worldly place. "It is absolutely essential that the thought and speech of each member in a community should accord with the rest, otherwise discord is detected, which sounds in the minds of others like a harsh grating noise. Furthermore, everything discordant is destructive of unity."

So, as we look through various segments of history, we see many writers echoing the idea of harmony and dissonance, and its relationship to the spirit world. In fact, it's a belief that is held to this day. As can be seen from these examples, the idea of an ongoing conflict between good and evil, between order and chaos, and between harmony and disharmony was prevalent for years. With this in mind, is it really a mystery as to why when musician's came to the United States with dissonant tunings, rhythms, and distorted musical instruments religious people were suspicious? Did it ever occur to musicians to consider listening to their critics?

On the other hand, did it ever occur to the critics that they should have more thoroughly analyzed the music so that they could have more rightly divided the divine gifts from the harmful elements that needed to be removed? As it was, they threw out the musical baby with the bathwater. Who knows what good might have happened if the critics would have encouraged the proper development of the talented instead of just ignorantly condemning everything and everyone.

Did it ever occur to those criticizing the musicians that perhaps they just needed a little bit of direction as to what they were to do with their divine talent? How many prayers were uttered for them? I highly suspect that very few prayers were said.

There are good questions that people on both sides of the argument should be asking themselves. Here are a few good questions that musicians and performers should ask themselves; Why is it that you want to be elevated up on a stage above everybody else? Why do you want to be elevated on a platform in front of everybody? Why do you want bright lights shining on you while all your brothers and sisters sit in the dark gazing admirably up at you as you stand on your pedestal? It's not necessarily wrong to be on a pedestal, a light isn't meant to be hidden under a bushel basket. It's put on a stand to give light. Are you giving light? Are you serving others? If you have a platform, use it to serve others. What are our motives and intentions for wanting to be musicians and performers in the first place? These are good questions for us to ask ourselves.

Here's a question the musician haters out in society may want to ask themselves; How is it that you can't honor the divine gifts in other people? If a person is living a wrong lifestyle and is using music in a wrong way, you should still be able to recognize the divine talent in that person and honor that talent, even if that person isn't acting honorable. It's alright that you discern the wrong and the bad in music. How is it that you can't discern and encourage the good?

Over the years there has been a lot of criticism of rock music. Honestly, it should be criticized. However, the problems span far beyond just rock music. Most country, jazz, pop, and some of what is called "gospel" music now use most of the same dissonant frequencies and beats as rock music. Yet many of the songs have some good mixed in with them.

This study isn't just targeting one type of music, it's targeting various problem areas within music in general. When it comes to music, It doesn't matter who you are. If you sow chaos and disorder, that's what you'll reap. If you sow harmony and order, that's what you'll get. The great thing is, you have a choice. If you find you're making mistakes, you can change what you are doing. You can choose to try to put orderly ingredients into your music. You can improve. Nobody is expecting you to be perfect immediately. It's something you can work towards. You can change your mind. This may take years to correct. It's highly unlikely you'll get it right immediately.

There is a large segment of the population that would describe the current world conditions as being very dark. At this time, we, as a people, need to more clearly understand the mindsets of people who are different from us. We need to understand their beliefs and ideologies.

You may not like somebody's religion or philosophy. It may seem like they are diametrically opposed to you in some of their ideologies. However, every now and then, they've thought of something that you have completely overlooked. On certain occasions, they are right and you are wrong. They've either spoken or written something that's 100 percent true. You need to get over it. They may be completely different from you, but on certain occasions they are correct. Be willing to admit it. It's the way to move forward.

One of the biggest topics that people have been stubborn about, is music. Over the years, we have witnessed certain religious people demonizing nearly every musician they've ever set their ears on. They don't seem to be able to discern the divine gifts and abilities latent within people. On the other hand, we've seen many recording artists who seem to have no regard for society, they won't listen to any constructive criticism. They don't at all mind bombarding the public with dissonant noise pollution just as long as their pockets are being filled with money. Many of them have demonstrated very little responsibility. Some of them have openly proclaimed themselves to be from the dark side. They're proud of it. Remember though, that you can't judge every modern songwriter by just a few evil individuals.

There is also a category of musicians and songwriters who produce a mixed product. Sometimes they are divinely inspired. Other times they may be inspired by evil. One song may be toxic and dissonant, and the very next one may be harmonious and divine. Just because a group or a songwriter has a few harmonious and inspired songs, it doesn't make every song they sing good. Nor, because they play some bad songs, does it automatically make every song they do bad. It just depends. Why does this happen? We are human beings. Human beings make mistakes. Other times people have sound judgment and make good decisions.

Music can reach heights beyond what has ever been reached before. Musicians should make a point of attempting to improve music. This is very difficult to do if religious people continue to demonize divine musical gifts when at times, the criticism isn't merited.There are other times that criticism is merited. Another factor that makes it difficult for music to reach its highest potential is if musicians keep creating toxic music. There is a tremendous need for balance in this art form.

Musicians have faced a lot of criticism over the years. However, what about all the good they do for society? The music business houses some of the most cordial people on the planet. Consider all the times they've lifted people's spirits with their music. What about all the concerts they've put on to raise money in order that food could be bought for hungry people? What about all the money they've contributed to various charities? What about all the effort musicians have put in to make people happy? Some of the musicians in the modern music business have done more in one day to help hungry and hurting people, than what entire groups of people have contributed in a lifetime. It is ironic however, that they do all these good things yet insist on bombarding people with non-harmonic sounds.

Let's face it, there are musicians who are a detriment to society. In such cases, is it possible that they can benefit from constructive criticism? Or, will they be too stubborn and ignorant to receive it? It would really be helpful if they would try to remove dissonance and improper tuning from their music. Within music is a greater potential for good. Perhaps it's not the answer to concentrate too often on the musical shortcomings of error prone human beings. Society in general has not seen what great things could happen if music was played more fully and commonly in its proper ways. This is true for all of the arts, not just music.

Chapter 15

The Unveiling Of A Vast Musical Structure

As we have mentioned, it appears as if modern music has displayed both good and evil. What can be learned from this? Is there a bigger picture? What is the grand scheme?

In an attempt to explain the overall perspective, let's build a word picture and make use of symbolism. Imagine if you will, that a marvelous musical structure has been under construction for thousands of years. The structure is not physical only, but is multi-dimensional. Although you can see some of this musical structure with your physical eyes, you can't see all of it. The only way that you can see the entire structure of which we speak is with a different set of eyes.

The eyes which are being referred to in this context are the eyes of the mind. The only way that the musical structure can be entirely comprehended is through word pictures which can be perceived by the mind.

Conceptualize that in order for this structure to come into its full manifestation, it has required millions of musical components to all meticulously come into place in the spirit world and on Earth over thousands of years. All of these intricate parts work together to reveal an epic musical reality. Envisage that the thousands of intricate parts of which we are speaking, are thousands of musicians who have lived out their lives during various time periods. They are people who have come to Earth and have expressed both good and bad musical attributes throughout the entire course of human history. As they have continued to come to Earth and live out their lives, and express their musical attributes, pieces of the musical puzzle fall into place, slowly revealing the big picture.

As we continue to construct a word picture within your imagination, visualize the following. Envision that the world we now live in is a reflective world. Within this reflective world, realities from a higher level are reflecting and playing themselves out in physical matter. There are many different kinds of realities coming into manifestation, other than just musical realities. Due to the fact that this study is on music, we will just concentrate on the musical realities.

During the Renaissance an artist depicted musical history as a structure that had been built through the ages. This is a picture called "The Temple of Sound". Each part of the building represents music history or a musical principle.

Imagine that in your mind's eye, you can see throughout the course of human history. In viewing all of human history, a great panorama has been set before your eyes. As time progresses, you continue to see in ever greater detail, that an unseen system of millions of spiritual musical archetypes has been in the process of exhibiting itself by becoming visible in the physical matter of this material world.

Over the course of time, an age-old musical reality which was previously unrecognized by human beings has been becoming encased in physical matter. This musical reality was first made known in the spirit world, but afterward, over a course of thousands of years, it has been emerging in physical reality on planet Earth.

As we continue with this word picture, you find that it's not at all hard to imagine that we have been witnessing the emergence of a vast musical structure. This isn't just a random structure that has its origins here on Earth. It has deeper origins. It has unfolded over the centuries. It first started unfolding in other dimensions. It then began materializing on planet Earth. As it has unfolded, we have seen both harmonious and disharmonious musicians. The purpose of the structure has been to transform the unseen musical polarities of a higher dimension, into physical matter so that they can be observed.

Where do archetypes come from? In real life we can see that thousands of different musicians have been made manifest on this planet. It may seem like a strange question to ask, but, why are they here? Where did they come from? What is the bigger picture? Why do some of them seem to be playing out musical villains and heroes? What are the answers to these types of questions that seldom get asked?

What started off in history with just a few musicians has grown into a huge structure. To use an analogy, it's as if a musical plant has grown out of a musical seed and has slowly unfolded to reveal all that was contained within it as it progressed over the centuries. Both harmonious and dissonant musicians have come forth in the world and have presented themselves.

Over the centuries we have seen people such as Pythagoras, John Sebastian Bach, Ludwig Beethoven, and others arise. They demonstrated order, harmony, and equilibrium in their compositions. There were also deep thinking philosophers and religious leaders who stressed orderly music in their societies. They viewed music as a sacred science. Were they just the earthly counterparts of harmonious musical beings from higher worlds?

On the other hand, there have been musicians who have claimed themselves Satanic. They have often demonstrated incoherent, and disharmonious noise. It's comical to hear them referring to themselves as composers, and calling their indecipherable noise, "compositions". They attempt to make a joke out of music without realizing that this is what they are doing. Ask yourself this question; Are these self proclaimed Satanic musicians just the earthly counterparts of disharmonious beings from another dimension? Are the musical events which we have witnessed on Earth just a reenactment of something that happened in another dimension a long time ago?

Conceptualize that these musical scenarios had to be played out over periods of thousands of years. Envisage that there was a reason that dark musicians had to be kept unaware of what they were doing. Part of the reason for the secrecy was, had they known the part they were playing, they may not have played it out. They had to play it out so that a revelatory musical panorama could be reenacted on the Earth. What if the events that could not be viewed by human beings because they had happened long ago in the spirit world, had to be made tangible in physical matter for human beings to see?

You have followed along by creating a word picture of these events in your mind to help you understand this concept. You are the one who decides what to do with this idea. Do you think that this concept conveyed to you by means of a word picture contains elements of the truth?

Consider the possibility that for centuries, the grand pageantry of all things musical has been displaying its various facets in physical matter. This grand musical structure displays vast musical contrasts. It materializes in physical matter, that which was witnessed by other types of beings in other realms. It brings unseen polarities into your awareness.

If one were to follow this line of thought, musicians on this planet would be seen in a different light. For example, spiritually minded men such as Bach and Beethoven wouldn't just be seen simply as people who composed music. They would be seen as symbols, archetypes, and representatives of a harmonious order which exists in the realms beyond. By contrast, modern noisemakers who openly proclaim themselves to be of the dark side, would be seen as the earthly counterparts of disharmonious beings from another dimension.

Chapter 16

The Hidden Side Of Light And The Next Genesis

The mindset of many seers, sages, and scribes has been one which strongly emphasizes the idea that the visible world set before us is only here to give us information about a world that we can't see, except on rare divine occasions. The tangible, physical, realities you can contact with your senses, are just reflectors of a reality that hides beyond the veil, and is imperceptible to your physical senses.

Here is another short recap. The way of thinking in many cultures for thousands of years has been this; In a prior spiritual world, there were two groups. There were those who were in harmony with divine order, and there were those who became beings of disharmony and disorder. Once again, be reminded that when we speak of harmony and disharmony within this context, we are speaking of harmony and disharmony that may have involved music, but actually goes way beyond it.

Then when you look at the moral stories that were told in cultures, which were not a part of religious thought, you find similar ideas. When you look at the archetypes of dark musicians, such as the one demonstrated by the pied piper story, you'll find that they aren't always immediately recognized as being musical villains. They often appear as being very witty and charming at first, perhaps even doing society some good. Then, as time progresses their true role is revealed. These types of villains would be the ones who don't openly proclaim themselves satanic.

These types of stories may reflect some of the deeper ideas people have had about the idea of evil in general. The general consensus concerning evil throughout history, is that it seeks to work covertly. Its desire is to operate undetected. The strategy of some musical villains is not to be purely evil. Rather, it is to be both good and evil. What generally happens, is that at some point in the story, their dark side is exposed. In speaking of how darkness is generally exposed, let's make use of another metaphor here.

We are all familiar with the idea of natural light. We know all about sunlight and what it accomplishes. When the sun rises in the morning, everything suddenly becomes apparent. It is a visible radiance that is detected by our senses. When it begins to shine in the morning it exposes physical structures that had been hidden and obscured by the darkness of the night.

Now let us examine a different type of light. There is also an invisible radiance which brings light to darkened hearts and minds. It is the hidden side of light. This hidden light can shine and reveal things that had been hidden from the heart and mind. Light in the area of music, would consist of vital information that brings a mental illumination concerning it.

This light is a real, invisible substance which is just as real as the invisible substances of air or electricity. When this light strikes the human mind, new realities are exposed to the mind in many different areas of life. So, in the topic of conversation, which would in this case be music, a light comes to the mind which reveals formerly undetected musical realities.

Earlier in the book, we made use of a picture story to try to explain a possible hidden musical reality. Let's revisit that idea to illustrate how the hidden side of light can strike the human mind and reveal a hidden reality. In keeping with the purposes of this book, we will keep the topic within the realms of music.

In creating another word picture here, imagine that invisible light strikes the mind, and a new musical reality emerges. Suddenly, a musical structure which has taken thousands of years to come into place, comes into view within your mind's eye. It was already there, but it suddenly comes into your field of awareness. It comes into view out of the invisible. It has been there, but a realization of it suddenly dawns within consciousness.

This centuries old illustration demonstrates the interplay between light and shadow. Throughout history this has been a common theme in symbolizing the contrast between good and evil.

This light of a different kind, unveils a vast musical structure on the spur of the moment. You suddenly see this structure as you begin to comprehend it. You comprehend it by means of your mind's eye. This structure lays out before you in detail the outworkings of an age-old, grand cosmic symphony. When the light of this special knowledge shines on this musical structure, it exposes a huge musical edifice which radiates understanding concerning the interplay of both harmony and disharmony. It has taken the entire history of the World for its components to come into place, so that a composite picture of all ages can come together and be seen.

Suddenly, you can see the musicians of light and musicians of darkness through the ages. You understand more fully the operations of the illuminated musicians of light and the unilluminated musicians of darkness. You see how they fit into the plan throughout history. How do the light and the darkness work together to bring you an understanding? Aren't they enemies? Well, yes, but the entire scenario still works at a higher level to give those who are supposed to see it a greater understanding. It works in a similar way to how pictures used to be developed in a photography darkroom. The negative and the positive have to come together in order for a true picture to emerge.

Over the centuries, a musical picture has been developing. It is a picture that illustrates how darkness was necessary in order for the light to be made manifest. Now that darkness is close to the point where it has run its course, it's time for the light to rise and completely destroy the darkness. It's getting closer to the time for harmony to come forth and completely swallow up disharmony.

The light of mental illumination breaks in upon the awareness of those who are supposed to know. It begins to be understood that all that happened in the entire history of this planet was just all a part of a brilliant musical master plan emanating from the mind of the Great Conductor of the universal symphony of all things.

Let's, at this point, briefly go back to the original symbolism used in the writing of this book. The major thought behind the symbolism of this book series is this; You are using your mental facilities to imagine that by considering the thoughts presented to you in the Starboard Quest books, you are climbing aboard a symbolic ship. The name of the ship is, "The Starboard Quest". You are going exploring, and the sea on which you journey is a sea of sound waves. The point by which you are navigating, is a certain constellation in the sky. The name of this constellation is Lyra. Lyra is an actual constellation, and in Hebrew astronomy it was depicted as being an upward ascending eagle with a harp as part of its body.

In this symbolism, the Lyra harp is symbolic of divine and harmonic music. In the symbolism, you, the reader, are navigating towards this constellation of perfect harmony and order. It is symbolic of your quest to understand the deeper harmonic realms of sound. Now let's add a deeper symbolism to this picture story. Let's say that all this time you thought this celestial harp was your destination. At some point in your quest, you discover something astounding! It ends up that the constellation was not your destination. It was only a sign, an emblem directing you to something greater! You discover that the mysterious something you thought you were navigating towards is someone. It is the Great Master Musician. It is the Divine Conductor of the universal symphony of all things.

The music being conducted by the Divine Conductor contains within it, the harmonic outworkings of everything that is. This includes all geometric forms, all mathematical cymatics, all times, all places, all creatures, all dimensions, all beings, all spiritual beings. Everything that ever has been or ever will be are contained within this timeless symphony. It is all one dynamic whole, one amazing orchestra. All that has ever existed or ever will exist are a part of this composition. All of it has been working towards an ultimate musical climatic and crowning zenith. It is a flawless symphony which is perfect in harmony, order, and beauty. It is a timeless symphony which has no beginning and will have no end. It is an entirely new octave which humans haven't even imagined yet.

Every day, the new octave is slowly emerging. The symphony is getting louder every day, but only for those who have ears to hear. The majority of the world's population can't hear it. Even those who by chance pick up the distant echoes of it, just ignore it. You see, the disharmonious creatures of this world are fighting the arrival of this music. It doesn't matter how much they fight it. It is slowly coming into our atmosphere. It is dawning within the consciousness of the few. It will bathe the ears of every regenerated being on the planet.

The symphony, and its supreme qualities are only reflections and echoes. They are ripples to the surface of something deeper. They are timeless waves of the music of the Supreme Master Conductor of the timeless orchestra.

Over the millenia, the musical scale has risen note by note. It is reaching towards the apex. Soon comes the new glorious and liberating octave. Unlike the present "scale" which contains both light and darkness, the new octave contains only light. It's a new genesis. What are the characteristics of a genesis? A genesis is when light comes forth out of darkness. It's when order comes forth out of chaos. It is when harmony emerges from disharmony. At the present moment, we are in a world of light and darkness. It's a world of good and evil, of harmony and disharmony. However, that which is slowly phasing in, is a world of light and harmony. There will be no darkness or dissonance in the coming world. This is the genesis of something new.

Do you begin to see the necessity of the destructive and willingly dissonant musicians who came on the scene in large numbers? Disharmony and dissonance are a part of the ingredients of darkness that needed to be present so that a genesis could take place. This is so that a higher order of love and harmony could come into manifestation and rise in triumphant glory over the disharmony. In other words, darkness has set the stage for the light to rise in victory over the darkness. As you know, darkness enhances the light.

The essence of music as it was in its origins before time and space, is perfect. In this world, the pure essence of music is like a seed. It's there somewhere, but imperfect people are handling it, and have been for centuries. The idea behind the progression of music is to let it unfold into all of its splendor and perfection. Despite the fact that evil people have tried to dirty this sacred science, this effort will not continue forever. It may have appeared to have worked for them for a short time, but this won't endure. Music's perfect manifestation is still in that original musical seed as it unfolds. One of the purposes of music is its regeneration back into its original magnificent condition. Every art and science can reach its full potential of being a great help for mankind if it continues to unfold from the seed of itself. It can achieve the full potential of itself. It was not created to do harm, it was created to do good.

As this musical seed grows into the tremendous potential that is inherent in it, it also devours its adversaries. It will eventually swallow up the "insects" which are attempting to prevent its perfection. As it ascends from one level of magnificent refinement to the next. It will expel and thrust off that which is incompatible with its fresh regeneration. At the same time, there is also a process ongoing, in which that which was previously not up to par can be transformed into the new musical essence. It is possible that some plants grow stronger due to some of the harmful conditions in their atmosphere that have threatened them. It is possible that the same is happening with the very essence of music. It is growing stronger due to some of the hostile musicians who have misused it.

Now arising, is the music of the Great Universal Super Being. His musical instrument consists of all harmonic reality. It consists of every harmonic element that ever has been or ever will be. It encapsulates all creatures, all creation, in all dimensions. The song is beginning to break through into this dimension. It will continue to, in an ever increasing manner. It grows like a mighty oak, it casts off all its hindrances. All that opposes this slow rising song, will be dissolved.

One note of the great symphonic beyond is more beautiful than any song ever sung by any angelic being or mortal. Throughout the ages, at special times, distant echoes of the music have come through. Now, it will come forth in an increasing manner.

Nature is beginning to tune its harps. There will be perfect harmony in every ray of light, in every speck of dust. What is being spoken of here, is the universal harmony of all things. It is in the slow process of arriving now. The song is rising. The new octave will come forth. The musical instrument being played is all reality. All creatures will be in perfect harmony. The stars in perfect harmony, the Earth in perfect harmony. The light arises. The disharmonious creatures run from the light and back to the darkness. The songs of humans can't even begin to approach what is coming.

This musical process can also be explained by using an analogy which utilizes the science of chemistry. Picture if you will, a scenario in which music is becoming perfected by time in the great chemistry lab of human history.

Let's suppose that musical polarities from eternity are being poured into the bottle of time, and the bottle is so big it contains the entire universe. Both musical light and darkness have been poured into this vast glass beaker. Trillions of cosmic chemical/musical reactions have taken place in the mixture through eons of time. The substances are all reacting with one another. Eventually, a radiant new musical essence will come forth. The conditions don't seem right. However, the hostile polarities will bring forth new musical realities. A fresh musical essence will be born out of the womb of musical chaos. Without this differentiation no good can result. It's a type of genesis. Light comes forth out of darkness. Order emerges from chaos. First there had to be chaos, it is the condition which is necessary to manifest musical order.

The entire universe, which embodies all the suns, moons, and planets can be thought of as a container. For the entire body of stars, the sum total of them, must be contained within something. For the purposes of our study on the music of planet Earth, let's narrow this study down to just our current world. In order to explain another concept, let's use another word picture.

Visualize if you will, the beautiful blue planet we are currently dwelling upon. Now picture the atmosphere which surrounds it as a bottle, or a container so to speak. The outer edge of the atmosphere, being as it were, the transparent walls of the bottle. Everything is contained within this bubble, or a type of glass beaker.

Every song ever sung in the history of the world, and every piece of music, good or bad that has ever been played has been poured forth into this container, poured forth into the air of planet Earth. In other words, all the music that has ever been made, is contained within this atmospheric bottle. It is self contained. In fact, scientists have discovered that no sound made is ever lost. The sounds just go deeper into the ether and circle around in the atmosphere of the Earth. This can be compared to the solution within a chemistry bottle being stirred in order to bring a new compound or essence to life.

All of the bad elements, which would be all of the dissonant music, are to be transmuted into good elements. The bad elements need to be destroyed in order to become food for the progress of the total solution. The outer forms need to be destroyed, annihilated, utterly dissolved, in order that any good essence within them may be released. In a similar way, all of the disharmonious music, with all of its backbeats, nonharmonic tunings, distortions, filthy and perverse lyrics, and the hedonistic, materialistic lifestyles that go along with this type of music is going to be completely and utterly consumed and destroyed. Something must die, in order that something new can live. Then the hope of Martin Luther for music will be realized.

It is through the natural processes of chemistry, that the bad and harmful elements are devoured. These harmful elements, being poured forth into the solution, which are completely dissolved are necessary for the development of the new compound. In order for the true essence, the new life to be released, We see this very plainly in the regeneration of a plant. When a seed is put into the ground, it must completely die and rot away in order that the new creation can come. Throughout the ages a mysterious musical tincture has been formulating.

In this giant musical process, there must come a dissolution of music such as we now know it. Rock, country, jazz, new age, folk, hip-hop, rap, and certain other types of music must perish. At the same time, if there is any remnant of good in this music, it must be spared. It's dissolution, or it's dissolving must come in order that the new may be born. Something new comes out of the death of the old. A musical phoenix must take place. A new music arises out of the ashes of the old. This type of process is happening in countless areas, and music is just one of the areas.

Universal truths can be found in all arts and sciences. Through studying such things as music, architecture, chemistry, mathematics, etc. we can learn. All of these arts and sciences follow universal and divine laws. There are eternal truths that are hidden behind the facts. The truth must be released from the forms.

All of the arts can be transformed into divine arts. From them, we can unlock the eternal essences which are above the material parts of them. Contained within the seven liberal arts may be hidden clues to inner transformation, for all arts operate by the unseen principles contained within creation.

Chapter 17

Battle of The Ages

Throughout the ages, scholars have recognized that all of creation is exhibiting musical ratios. All of creation is vibrating. Mathematically speaking, it is a form of music. Scientists have even discovered that the sun is making music. They have demonstrated that the magnetosphere of planet earth is acting in the capacity of a giant musical instrument.

In a Boehme type mindset, these could be just a couple of examples demonstrating how a hidden song has been secretly latent in all creation. According to ancient sages,one of the great events that we have been heading towards for thousands of years is a time when selected and elected beings will be interfaced directly back into a divine and supernatural universal instrument of perfect harmony. As every component of this instrument comes into place, the Master Musician, the Universal Super Being will play the entire creation as one harmonious instrument. This is an incredible idea, but once again be reminded that this is an idea that has been around for a long time and you are going to have to decide what you are going to do with this information. According to this train of thought,the universe is in harmony with the plan, but human beings are out of harmony. Since human beings have stepped away from harmony, they can't hear the divine music. However, this harmony will dawn, and is dawning in the consciousness of a few.

Let's look into the idea of the harmony arising in the consciousness of the few. Harmony arising in consciousness, is the result of inner harmony. It comes from peace within the heart. Perhaps the reason that there is so much imbalance and distortion, dissonance and perversion in the music of the modern times, is because it is the reflection of a lack of harmony from within people. In contrast to this, the orderly masterpieces of the past were simply a reflection of their inner harmony and peace of mind. Once again, coming to the surface of humanity are ripples from the past from the cosmic conflict between harmony and disharmony. In order to explain this in more detail let's draw some inspiration from a few of the brilliant artisans from the past. Art and music are directly related, so in this case an examination of a few magnificent artists will be drawn upon.

It is known that Leonardo Davinci often incorporated the golden proportion into his paintings. He used sacred geometry in the layout of some of his works. In doing this, he was in a sense respecting the unseen laws of reality. He used certain proportions and mathematical angles in his drawings. He was a man of character and integrity. His art was a reflection of his obedience to universal law. His art demonstrated discipline, perseverance, and patience. He had inner harmony and inner peace. His harmonious art was the reflection of his own inner harmony.

Now let's implement the law of contrast. Compare the art of Leonardo Davinci, to the art of someone in the world today who calls themselves an artisan, the creator of modern "art". The "art" that these types of "artists" create may consist of something similar to the following. Let's say for instance, that someone has taken a raw hunk of cow manure and smeared it around on a canvas in a random manner. A badly written poem is attached to it. The exhibit is open to interpretation. One person says that it looks to them like a dog. Another says it looks like a cat. This act is an open insult to the very nature of art. Yet, if people are subjected to art like this for long enough, they will eventually be convinced that it is beautiful. They will pay high prices for it, and gather into intellectual circles to talk about this type of "art". The person who spread the manure on the canvas will be considered a celebrity. At the same time, the art of Michael Angelo, Leonardo Davinci, and others will be considered inferior. The modern "art" that was created by the "celebrity" is simply the reflection of a twisted mind, and of someone who has no inner harmony. They were too lazy to put time and effort into it. They wanted to be "artistically spontaneous".

However, despite this fact, the modern "art" has served a purpose, and part of what has been accomplished is that a greater appreciation of true good art is fostered by means of the badness of the modern "art". This is called the law of contrasts. You can not know what good is unless you know what bad is. It takes a bad piece of art to know what good art is. However, those creating the bad art, will never admit that some other art is actually better. What they will do, is they will form social networks composed of disharmonious people who have the same warped minds that they do. Then, together with all the people in their warped social network, they'll close their eyes to all art superior to their own.

Looking into the world of music we see the same type of thinking. There have been many brilliant composers throughout history. However, they will not be listened to or considered by many people in the modern day. Why? Because many people today have a warped sense of what good music is. Many of the modern radio stations are programmed by people with this warped sense of what good music is. What is being demonstrated a large portion of the time is really bad "music". This dark type of atmosphere is actually necessary for light to eventually emerge out of it. Once again, we would not know what harmonious music was, unless we were first exposed to an ample amount of dissonant and obnoxious music. You see, it's all subtle reflections of events from thousands of years ago taking place once again in the perpetual cycles. Order must once again emerge from chaos.

There is a master plan for music that has been working itself out through the ages. True divine science, and the arts are here to make us better. There are heavenly laws behind all of these artistic endeavors that we are supposed to be learning. They aren't here to just prosper us materially.

In a type of thinking similar to Boehme's, it could be seen that a large number of people on this Earth, being either possessed by, or strongly under the influence of disharmonious beings, don't want this musical master plan to come to pass. They are fighting this event, as others have been for hundreds of years. They are at war with the music of the spheres, but they don't know it. Many of them have completely given themselves over to disharmony. However, even though they are in this state, some can be liberated. There is still hope. Then the liberty bells of true music will ring.

Pythagoras, Plato, and many other sages have implied that we stand at the thresh-hold of a doorway that leads into a harmonious and glorious world. Their belief was that the dissonant will not walk through this doorway and into this harmonic world. Rather, they will increase their disharmonic ways, ignore the new reality, and fight its arrival.

So according to people like Jacob Boehme, what we are dealing with is a figurative musical battle. In his way of thinking, millions of human beings are being "played" by large numbers of disharmonious spirit beings. According to his ideas, only a small minority of humans are being played in a harmonious way. Thus, once again the villains outnumber the heroes, but the heroes will overcome. The impulse or rhythm by which the disharmonious live and conduct their lives and their music is contrary to nature.

If you are considering the possibility of some of these ideas, you may be asking the following question; I believe that something similar to this may be happening, but If it is, then why isn't it more obvious? It may be because the disharmonious beings that are playing disharmonious people want to remain undetected. This way, they can keep everything out of universal harmony without the human race knowing about it. As has been mentioned earlier, there was a belief prevalent in former times that human beings are like musical instruments. Each person is being played by one side or the other in a spiritual battle. Actually, human beings can fall under the influence of either side. A great shift is coming to the orchestra of the world, some musicians on this Earth don't want it to come. They are fighting a losing battle. The new song can not be held back forever. The return of the great symphonic beyond is inevitable.

Chapter 18

A Musical Call to Future Generations

We stand at the threshold of great world change. You are invited to be a part of the catalyst which could help set off a planet wide musical revolution. This revolution, being set in motion, could help restore harmony to the world. Although, before the harmony of this new octave comes forth, this present world system will pass away. Above mankind rests a dark sky, but within that dark sky are millions of bright constellations. There is an incredible fuel which feeds as many suns as there are grains of sand on the shores of the sea. Those suns all demonstrate musical harmony and shed light into the dark sky.

Ancient sages have told us that there is a harmony of the elements. That is why there is a relationship between music notes, planets, and light waves. One age-old idea that reflects this, is the thought that every star in the sky has its counterpart in a flower on the Earth.

Let us awaken the sleeping giant. The sleeping giant in this context is symbolic of the great unrealized musical power and potential lying dormant in the rare individuals who are willing to help bring in harmonious music. For many years, the great musical talent in the common people has been left sleeping beneath the dark musical sky. This is because only the talents of just a few artists have been predominantly pushed upon the listening ears of the masses by record companies and media. It would certainly appear as if many of the people who have run the entertainment business have been highly influenced by the disharmonious. It would be wonderful if some of the elite in the music business would have a change of heart. Many would be happy about this. Some of them have had a change of heart.

The great harmonious musical potential of those who will be taught the proper purposes of music needs to be unleashed upon mankind. The full potency of music rightly applied needs to be brought forth. Much of music should first be purged of its toxic elements. Society needs to be freed from the musical mistakes that have continued unchallenged for decades. The human race needs to be liberated from some of the toxic music that has imprisoned it in darkness for years.

Audible music as we've known it in recent times, has predominantly catered to the physical senses. It has not always been this way. Composers such as Bach tried to use music to liberate the people into a place beyond material reality. Music which currently is being played many times seeks to cater to people's animal instincts. In doing so, it captivates people in their lower natures. During the musical performances of those making music that cater to the peoples lower nature, are we witnessing thousands of poor souls attending those performances who are prisoners of their lower natures? If so, these people need to be liberated from their captivity. They need to be liberated from these so- called "musicians". The musicians themselves need to be liberated from themselves.

Yes, it's time to do away with as many of the dark elements found in modern music, as is possible. At the same time, all of its good and noble qualities need to be preserved and refined. It's time to step out of chaos and into a greater order. If we attempt to do this, will the music be perfect? No, that's not what's being implied. There will most likely be plenty of mistakes in it, but at least we will be moving in a better direction. All of our attempts to do better with our human music, won't even come close to the coming super music spoken of by ancient sages. However, we can demonstrate a willingness to try to do better with what we have now. Most likely, the very best we accomplish will still be far below divine standards, but at least a gallant effort can be put in.

It is inevitable, that in elect persons, an amazing transformation can take place, and is taking place. This is an amazing transformation process that has been ongoing for ages. This is a unique process of chemistry in the laboratory of Planet Earth in which light can emerge out of darkness. Health can arise out of sickness. Harmony out of dissonance. Order can emerge from chaos. It is the ascension into the new octave.

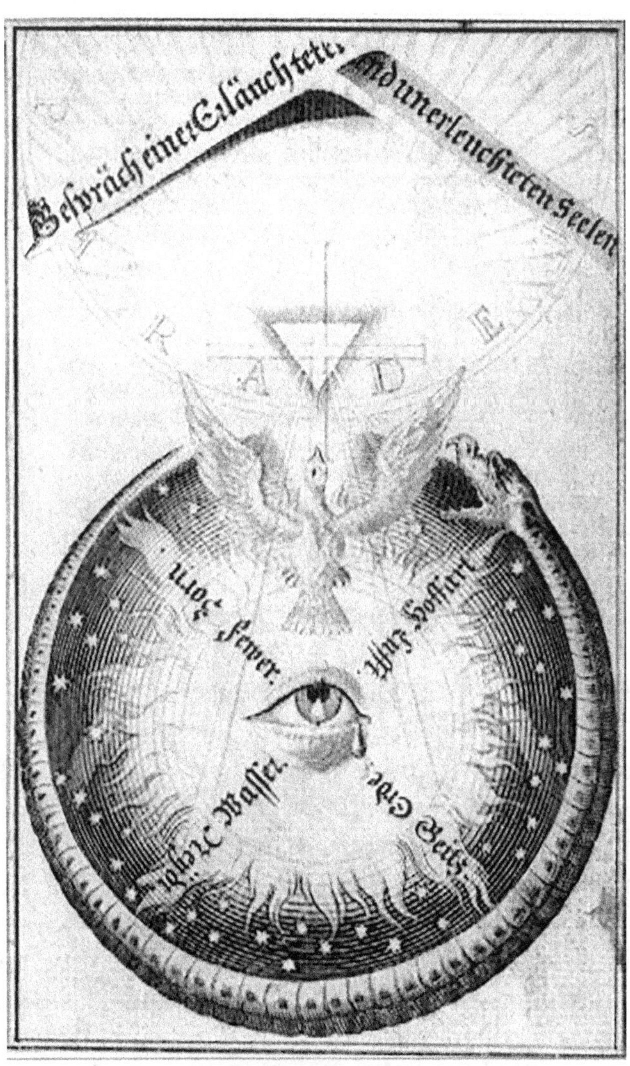

This picture from centuries ago seems to be depicting the concept of ascension.

A call goes out to all of those who want to try to move in the direction of trying to phase out of the primitive disorderly noise we have so often been subjected to. Now, and in the future, we can attempt to make wiser decisions. We can be more intelligent about our musical choices. It's time to try to rise above the bad elements. We can do better.

The time periods that were allotted for many of the different dissonant genres of music we have known is coming to an end. Perhaps there were a few good elements that were in at least some of them that we can take with us into the future. It's time for an expanded awareness of music's positive potential. It's time to contribute to the positive metamorphosis of music. Restore harmony to the world! Restore it in music, in relationships, in your diet, in your lifestyle, and in every area of life that harmony is missing. Although it is true that human effort can't really accomplish this, doing the best we can demonstrates the willingness to make an attempt at it.

It seems as if in the last number of decades music has gotten into the hands of some of the most vile and contemptible people who have ever walked the face of this Earth. There are also some very good and decent people in the business, but many of the others have used their power in the wrong way. They've influenced people to harm their bodies and wreck their lives. We've got several generations of drug addicts that are the result of this. Don't worry, though, this was all preknown. It has been for a purpose. At the same time, we don't have to just sit back and let it happen like we have in former decades.

We ought to do away with drug music. Don't support bands who use drugs recreationally. What is needed is a complete departure from the entire drug culture and mindset. For many years the hippie culture claimed a monopoly on music. Some of their behaviors have caused the question to arise; Has there ever been a more unworthy class of people to indulge in such a sacred science? It's as if they are mocking a sacred science. They show very little of the character as was demonstrated by such men as Martin Luther or John Wesley, and other excellent songwriters.

At the same time, you have to admire the hippie culture in the sense that most of them opposed war, they realized society needed a greater connection to the environment and they promoted green energy. These are all good things that could be taken with us into the future. It's time to retain what was good from the past, get rid of what was bad, and move forward into the future.

The young generation has to be encouraged to be smarter than many of their predecessors in regards to what they contribute to society in regards to what music they create for people. They can set their sights on an elevated music that will contribute a greater good to the people of this planet. At the same time, they can appreciate the good that former generations contributed, while avoiding their mistakes.

One area that the upcoming generations should consider, is that of strengthening sexual gender. The Greeks thought that non principled music in certain modes would make people androgynous. There are some that may argue with that, but take a look at a picture of men and women back in the 1940s before modern music came in. Then, take a look at them now. Although it can't be proven that the music had anything to do with this, it does raise the question.

It's time to forgive those who have made mistakes with their music. It's also time to part company with those who purposely want to live unharmonious lives. They do so themselves, and encourage others to do the same. They do this with both their lifestyles and their music. Many of the record companies and musicians at both a professional and independent level have become detrimental to the sacred rite of music. Don't put up with it.

Why has this been allowed? Stand up and be counted! Bring true tones and harmony to the world. Restore order to the chaos brought to this planet by disharmonious musicians and their fans.

Chapter 19

Where To Go Next

You may be asking, If we do need to change music, where do we begin? A great first step may be to restore harmony to the world. Harmony needs to be restored to every sphere of life imaginable. Some of these areas are; harmony in relationships, harmony in marriages, harmony in financial areas, social harmony, political harmony, ecological harmony, and economic harmony. These are just a few out of many. There are literally thousands of areas of life that balance, harmony, melody, and perfect timing need to be restored and rejuvenated in. You may be thinking, what do all these areas have to do with music? Probably a lot more than what you think. In ancient cultures, music was believed to be a reflection of the general atmosphere of the culture. Perhaps this is why we've had so much dissonant music for so many decades now. It's a reflection of the culture. We need deep and honest spirituality, clean air, clean water, healthy foods, healthy sound vibrations, great relations between parents and children, and harmony in multiple areas restored. Then perhaps, the atmosphere of these conditions will be reflected in the music. Actually, what is being spoken of here, is not, in one sense of the word, a call to peace. It's a call to war. It's a call to division. Fight the evil in society. Don't just go along with the disharmony.

Some of the greatest musicians who have ever walked the face of the Earth may have never yet even picked up a musical instrument. Perhaps they see the caliber of some of the people currently involved in the music industry and want nothing to do with it? I would encourage these people to reclaim music. Actually, according to ancient thought, nearly everything is a form of music. The true musician should seek to restore music and promote harmony in all areas of life. They should be ambassadors of harmony at every level. If you aren't a musician, you can still be an agent of harmony in other areas of life. In that way of thinking, you are a musician.

The idea of eliminating noise pollution is a great one. However, noise pollution goes far beyond the conventional idea of noise pollution. A good share of what people say and the music they play is full of cursing and negativity. You can call it freedom of speech, but really what it is, is a worse form of noise pollution than industrial noise pollution. Another good starting point would be to eliminate all the cursing and negativity from music.

The healing power of art, chromotherapy, herbs, and music should be paired correctly and used together to promote well being. Think of it as a sonic multi-vitamin. Over a period of time, not only has a lot of the music been disharmonious, but many of the musicians playing this type of music have been dissident as well as dissonant in other areas of life as well. Many of them have promoted hedonistic lifestyles, rebellion against parents, rebellion against spirituality, they've promoted drug use, violence, and have helped produce a bunch of weak minded people. In the case of such people isn't it time to instigate a mass sonic exorcism?

Composers should work hand in hand with scientists, astronomers, mathematicians and truly spiritual people to bring the most beneficial frequencies, melodies, notes and rhythms into music. Will mistakes be made, yes. However, trying to move into musical idealism will be a plus in and of itself, even if a lot of mistakes are made. There's nothing wrong with shooting for perfection. Some people are worried about ai music. Don't be worried about it, use it as a tool to bring music to a greater level.

Negativity should be removed from music. Words should be uplifting and contemplative. They should teach moral lessons. They should do some kind of good for people.

As far as some of the actual elements going into music, here are some suggestions. Why not place beneficial frequencies discovered by Dr. Royal Raymond Rife into compositions? How about removing backbeats and stopped antiseptic beats from music? Why not implement Pythagorean tunings? Natural rhythms of Earth and the universe could be used instead of backbeats. Left/ right brain synchronization could come to play in music. Above all, musicians should want to be filled with divine love. Even if they aren't at the moment.

Instead of having thousands of musicians milling about without jobs simply because they think they have to be entertainers, the mindsets could be refocused. They could be trained as music therapists. This would be much better than them pursuing unrealistic goals. They could be trained in the right ways and be taught to use the correct frequencies. Their talents could be put to use helping humanity. This would be much better than them trying to make it in a business that really does not profit them. Jobs could be created, and they could earn a great income.

Perhaps some of the musically inclined could go into vibrational medicine. Instead of just being another mediocre performer, they could do some real good in the world. New schools could be opened. Thousands of jobs could be created. Doctors and musicians could work together to create more healthy music.

Quite some time ago, a health food revolution began. People began making more healthy decisions with their eating habits. They began eating more natural foods. Today the health food industry is thriving, and is worth billions of dollars. The same thing may be in process with the music industry. People are listening to more and more music which is composed using healthy vibrations. Imagine if instead of people being bombarded with toxic music, they were engulfed on a continuous basis with healing music.

Not every piece of music over the last few decades has been toxic. There are some masterpieces mixed in with all the rest of the songs as well. There has been a mix of both good and bad, often from the same performers. Musicians have had the freedom to make mistakes. That's understandable, we all do. That being said, why not keep the good and get rid of the bad, at least to the extent of what we know to do?

We are getting closer and closer to a new kind of music everyday. You may not have noticed it, but we are heading towards a new octave. We will arrive at a place where the arts will maintain their integrity. No longer will there be such a glorification of materialism, or terrible art and music.

Another behavior that can be observed in the disharmonious, is that they publicly encourage and promote lives of lavish materiality. There is an attitude that creativity and music is predominantly for the youth and for helping to supply a life of excess materialism.These are also lies that people should be encouraged to not put up with anymore. Sometimes an older, more experienced composer can come up with a masterpiece that is superior to those who are younger. The young and the old should get together more often to benefit one another. A unique chemistry can be enacted. The youth can benefit from the wisdom and the experience of the elderly, while the elderly can benefit from the energy and invigorating enthusiasm of the youth. The rich and the poor should make music together, as well as the famous and the common. We should get rid of the idea of celebrity. Everyone is a celebrity in their own way.

Chapter 20

❦ ❧

Where Everything Is Really Headed

In summary, many brilliant sages throughout the centuries have told us that the planets are moving in a musical way throughout our solar system. Just as music is an invisible power that sometimes makes us want to tap our feet, there is unseen music of a higher order that makes the planets want to dance throughout the solar system. Throughout time, sages have called this music "The Music Of The Spheres". Some have thought of it as the greatest music there is. However, there is a greater music beyond all the influences of this material reality.

Many ancient cultures and religions stressed the importance of having orderly music in their societies. There was a deeply ingrained belief that harmonious order was good and that chaotic dissonance was evil. Most cultures have had the common belief in musical villains and heroes.

Modern scientists are studying frequency, sound, and vibration and are beginning to find out that some of the musical ideas that ancient sages had were more scientific than what modern researchers had previously realized. Some of the ideas of the sages are being proven true. A good example of this is found in the fact that scientists have discovered in the last number of years that the sun and the magnetosphere of the Earth are acting in the capacity of gigantic musical instruments. There are most likely millions of other celestial spheres operating in a similar way that haven't been discovered yet. There is a tremendous interest in frequency, sound, and vibration at this current time.

It's as if people can sense within their subconscious minds that there is an understanding on its way concerning it. It's as if all of this fascination in the area of frequency, sound, and vibration are pointing towards a greater oncoming revelation concerning it. There's something in the air.

Studies in the areas of cymatics, harmonic resonance, frequency, sound, and vibration are uncovering amazing things. Research into the 432 hertz frequency continues to confirm the importance of that number in regards to its relationship to the Earth and the universe. A close examination reveals an ongoing battle between harmonious and disharmonious beings that has lasted from before the foundation of the world to the present moment.

It is quite obvious that the entire universe is a profound harmonic structure. It would be hard to imagine that a harmonic structure of such great magnitude, one that reveals such precision and exactitude in exhibiting musical proportions and mathematics in its movements, didn't have a major goal or destination. Just as a music scale has a major destination which it is aspiring to, which is called the new octave, so does our solar system.

In concluding this book, it's as if we've reached a harbor as we've taken our journey on the sea of sound. Remember, all of this knowledge that has been poured into you as you have read this book, needs to go a step further than just your mind. It will do you no good to just simply absorb the knowledge of others into your mind to be understood with the intellect only. A further process of chemistry must take place within you. What you should hope for, is that something in these words will help you unlock the hidden potential of music within you. It's the release of a pure inner substance that you should be aiming for by studying this book.

You can't really get an answer from anybody else. They may have it, but they can't unveil it to you. You can take everything that you have seen or heard from others on the outside, and let it stimulate your own programmed inner truth. It's the release of what certain peculiar people have on the inside that's the true essence. That's where the true music is.

Nearly all of the performers who are now well known in the world will be gone 100 years from now. Their concerts and recordings will most likely be all but forgotten. Life will have moved on and there will be very little interest, if any, in what is now popular music. Most of the radio stations that are currently being listened to by millions of people will be completely forgotten by that time, that is, if the world systems aren't already completely destroyed. There may be a radio personality mentioned in some historic record somewhere, in some dusty old record book that has not been taken off the shelf for years. Many of the celebrities who are now very respected, may not be by that time, when it is proven how primitive today's music actually was. However, those who are a part of the eternal symphony of the Master Conductor will sing and play for endless ages. For in the end, all that remains are the songs of heaven.

This book is most likely for just a few people in the world. It may end up in the hands of millions, but it's still just for the few. You could call those few "The Royal Society of Stellar Musicians." For those ready to sail further forward on the sea of sound, here is a very interesting metaphor for you. The actual names of the notes in a music scale are words that denote an ascension from Earth to heaven. They imply a transcendent journey from being an earth bound mortal creature to becoming an elevated eternal being. The arrival at a new octave, is signifying a new birth, in an elevated world. This can be taken at an individual level, wherein a few people will arrive at an elevated station, or it can be understood as being a new planetary level, in which planet Earth itself arrives at a new octave, as an exalted world. However, there is yet another amazing series of thoughts for you to consider that goes beyond the arrival of the planet at a fresh world octave.

Here are some final thoughts for you to ponder and consider as you sail forward on the sea of sound. Perhaps what you are about to read has something to do with a new universal octave the ancients believed all things are headed for. Several times in this book, the constellation

Lyra has been mentioned. There are those who believe it to be a symbol which is directly connected to universal divine harmony.

Here are a few interesting facts about Lyra. Lyra, the harp of divine harmony, is 25 light years from Earth. That is around 147 trillion miles away. If you divide 147 trillion by 340,277,777,778 it equals 432. In other words, the constellation Lyra is distanced from the Earth in a multiple of 432. The visible formation of the constellation is the shape of a parallelogram connected to a triangle. This may hold some secrets for those of you who are experts in the field of sacred geometry.

Within Lyra, is the well known Ring Nebula. The ring is expanding at a rate of 32,400 miles per hour. Which means of course, that it is expanding in a multiple of the number 432 (432 x75=32,400). Earlier in the book it was mentioned that in the world today, there seems to be a universal force working in the collective consciousness of the human race. There has been a resurgence of interest in frequency, sound, and vibration. A wide variety of people from different fields seem to have a profound interest in how math and the universe are connected to music. People seem to be subconsciously able to detect that there's something happening vibrationally. Perhaps the following fact will shed some light for you, on why this may be.

Here is one final fact for you to consider, and apply to the chemistry of your thought processes in relation to the various musical topics we have been considering in this book. Scientists have discovered where everything in this solar system is headed. It is headed directly towards the constellation Lyra, which is the constellation symbolized by the divine harp of perfect harmony. It is heading there fast, at 12 miles per second, which by the way, is……. 43,200 miles per hour. As has been mentioned, the constellation Lyra is just a marker, it's pointing to someone greater. The great Conductor of the divine symphony of all things.

Further Information

If you'd like to order the other books in the Starboard Quest book series, first check your local stores, if they aren't available there, order through Amazon or any other major bookseller worldwide.

The books available in The Starboard Quest book series are:

The Starboard Quest- Sailing The Sea Of Sound To Explore Music's Connection To The Universe

The Starboard Quest- Treasure Hunt

The Starboard Quest- The Harmonic Battle Of Evermore

To see other Starboard Quest products or to read Starboard Quest educational articles visit the Starboard Quest web site at; starboardquest. com (press the three gray bars at the top left to see all of your options)

To watch Starboard Quest music videos, watch Starboard Quest research videos, or to hear about Starboard Quest radio coverage or radio interviews go to the Starboard Quest YouTube channel @ starboardquest1005. In regards to the music videos, there is something you need to understand. Various music promotion companies were used to promote the videos. There is reason to believe that some of the views on YouTube were not legitimate. There is reason to believe that a good number of the views were bots. Keep this in mind, there are most likely far less viewers of the videos than what the numbers are indicating. Remember this when you are promoting your own videos. Make sure you get good companies that will actually support you.

The question of where to begin when attempting to create music with a deeper connection to the laws and mathematics of the universe is a good one. We have done a number of experiments. If you'd like to see what has been incorporated into some of these soundscapes go to starboardquest.com and click on the song titles. A full explanation will come up for each composition. You will be able to read some of the principles and procedures that went into the music structures.

For music only, check all your favorite electronic media such as I tunes, Pandora, Deezer, and etc. Remember, these music compositions are experiments, no claims are being made. We ourselves have probably made many mistakes with these compositions. On the surface, the sound recordings may not sound any different from much of the music you have already heard. If you are curious about what it is that makes them special, take a look into what goes into their structure by looking at the liner notes.

Here are examples from a couple of the latest compositions. In the piece of music entitled, "Into The Deep Blue" here are some of its ingredients. The song was recorded with Pythagrean tuning. Its speed was set at 108 bpm, which is one quarter of 432. Its rhythm consists mainly of thunder crashes and waves. There is a method implemented into the recording which is designed to help bring about left/right brain synchronization. The song is laid out according to the golden proportion. At the golden proportion point, you will hear morse code come in. This is an actual secret message for you to decipher. The cries of seagulls are actually part of the recording. You can hear that they are placed in perfect timing with the recording.

Another example is the piece entitled, "Zodiac Carousel" This composition was played in Pythagorean tuning. Its timing was also at 108 bpms. If you listen carefully, you will hear that the main rhythm is hoof beats. At three minutes and thirty seconds into the piece, the second chorus comes in with choirs. This point marks the golden proportion part of the song.

It is not being implied that these sound experiments are the aquarian music spoken of by the ancients. However, they may contain certain elements in them which are. Hopefully they will offer some inspiration to those of you who are super talented out there. View these recordings as seeds, which being planted may one day result in inspiring others to take these types of ideas a step further. I would be interested in seeing what you come up with based on some of the standards and principles presented in this series of books. Consider the Starboard Quest compositions the seeds of a new creative way of looking at sound.

If you'd like to assist with Starboard Quest research, or have any other comments or questions, want some consultation, or are interested in hiring me for speaking engagements on the topics in the book series, it would be wonderful to hear from you at starboardquest@gmail.com

Sails up! Anchors away!

There is more to explore!

Visit starboardquest.com

Follow on Facebook

Make sure you read,
"Starboard Quest, Sailing The Sea Of Sound To Explore Music's Connection To The Universe" and listen to its soundtrack

Listen on YouTube

"In a nutshell, perhaps the simplest explanation for the Starboard Quest concept is that it is a musical message in a bottle for the future."
-THE BOSTON HERALD-

"Music which compels people to gaze inward, introspect, and make a positive change within their lives."
-Minnesota Public Radio-

"Based on mathematics, set patterns, designs, and musical theory, this form of music is deeply entwined with information that is connected with astronomy, geometry, history, and mathematics."
- U.S. and Canada Report-

"Music that breaks free from the norms set in stone in society."
-Universal News Report-

As heard on;

National Public Radio- United States	*Radio Disney*
BBC Radio- Europe	*Billboard*
Sirius Satellite Radio	*Candid Radio*

AND MORE!